DARWIN'S

VICTORIAN MALADY

Evidence for its

Medically Induced

Origin

JOHN H. WINSLOW

DARWIN'S VICTORIAN MALADY

Memoirs of the
AMERICAN PHILOSOPHICAL SOCIETY
Held at Philadelphia
For Promoting Useful Knowledge
Volume 88

DARWIN'S VICTORIAN MALADY

EVIDENCE FOR ITS
MEDICALLY INDUCED ORIGIN

JOHN H. WINSLOW

Department of Geography-Anthropology

California State College

AMERICAN PHILOSOPHICAL SOCIETY

INDEPENDENCE SQUARE • PHILADELPHIA

1971

Copyright © 1971 by The American Philosophical Society

Library of Congress Catalog
Card Number 70–161989

ACKNOWLEDGMENTS

I would like to express my deep appreciation to the Research Corporation of New York City for its financial support, and to Charles Schauer (Research Corporation) for his assistance in many considerate ways. My thanks also to Dr. David R. Stoddart, Department of Geography, Cambridge University, and to Dr. C. H. Hine, Clinical Professor of Environmental and Occupational Medicine and Toxicology, San Francisco Medical Center, University of California, for reading the manuscript and offering their comments. I also appreciate the helpfulness of Mr. P. J. Gautrey and other members of the staff of the University Library, Cambridge University, and to Lester Hazell and Jan McVicar of Corta Madera and Castro Valley, California.

J. H. W.

CONTENTS

DARWIN'S VICTORIAN MALADY

INTRODUCTION

O N OCTOBER 14, 1837, exactly one year to the day after H. M. S. *Beagle* had moored at Plymouth at the end of its second surveying expedition, Charles Darwin wrote a letter to his old friend Professor Henslow outlining the reasons why he did not wish to accept the secretaryship of the Geological Society. One of the reasons was the state of his health (F. Darwin, 1888: **1**: pp. 286–287):

> My last objection is, that I doubt how far my health will stand the confinement of what I have to do, without any additional work. I merely repeat, that you may know I am not speaking idly, that when I consulted Dr. Clark in town, he at first urged me to give up entirely all writing and even correcting press for some weeks. Of late anything which flurries me completely knocks me up afterwards, and brings on a violent palpitation of the heart.

His health did not improve and he moved from Cambridge to London, and then, in September of 1842, to a secluded house outside of the village of Down. While in London he had also been under the care of Dr. (Sir) Henry Holland (*ibid.*, p. 301), a relative through both sides of his family, with whom he shared a number of common interests, including the question of the origin of species.[1] Dr. Holland thought highly of Sir James Clark's

---

[1] Holland's comments on the subject are very interesting. In his book, *Medical Notes and Reflections,* whose second edition was printed in 1840, he stated (1840: p. 12):

"The greater exactness of modern observation is ever placing before us new and wonderful instances, in which the most minute peculiarities or defects, in structure and function, are transmitted from one generation to another. Scarcely is there an organ or texture in the body, which does not give its particular proof of these variations, so transmissible:—and we might almost doubt the permanence of the type of our species, thus largely and unceasingly infringed upon, were we not permitted to see something of those more general laws, by which the Creator has set limits to the change, and made even the deviations subservient to the welfare of the whole."

A little later he made the following remarks in a footnote:

"Still we are not entitled to deny the followers of Geoffroy St. Hilaire the *possibility* that it may be otherwise; and that research may hereafter disclose to us some evidence that species are not immutable. If this were eventually proved to be so,

1

work on the relationship of disease to climate and physical environment (Holland, 1840: pp. 352, 458, 463), and it is very likely that the Dr. Clark mentioned in Darwin's letter to Professor Henslow was this same person.[2]

Darwin's decision to move from London to the country probably reflects the influence of both of his doctors. They shared a belief in the importance of environmental factors in the production or modification of disease, and both wrote on the subject. As an example the fourth edition of Dr. Clark's book, *The Sanative Influence of Climate,* had this to say (1846: pp. 1, 3, 78–79):

> The marked improvement in the health, produced by a change from the city to the country, even for a short period, and the great amelioration, and even cure, of various diseases effected by a removal from one part of the country to another, are matters of daily remark. It may suffice to mention, in reference to this fact, intermittent fevers, asthma, catarrhal affections, whooping-cough, dyspepsia, and various nervous disorders. These diseases are often benefited and not unfrequently cured, after having long resisted medical treatment, by simple change of situation; or they are

it would in no wise affect the great argument of Natural Theology. A law presumed at one time to be universal, would be found collateral or subordinate to a still higher law; further removed, it may be, from our comprehension of its details, but involving the same proofs of design as the basis of the whole."

He then went on to discuss the importance of the inheritance of "monstrosities" and the stages of development of the human embryo. It would seem not unlikely that he may have had some influence on the development of the thinking of his young relative and patient. There was probably no naturalist at that time whom Darwin knew who was as open-minded about the question. In 1859, soon after the publication of the *Origin of Species,* Darwin wrote to Thomas Huxley praising him for his help in winning over Sir Henry to the cause. His opinion of Holland's intellectual capacity was not high at the time, however (F. Darwin, 1888: **2**: pp. 223, 251). This may have been partly due to an earlier experience he had had with the Doctor as a critic—Sir Henry was one of the first persons to read the journal Darwin had kept on board the *Beagle* and he expressed the opinion that it was not worth publishing (see Litchfield, 1915: **1**: p. 247). Many years later, Darwin wrote to Alfred Wallace that the only one of his friends to speak out in favor of his theory of pangenesis was Henry Holland: he ". . . found it very tough reading, but admits that some view 'closely akin to it' will have to be admitted" (F. Darwin and Seward, 1903: **1**: p. 301).

[2] George M. Gould (1903: **1**: p. 98), W. W. Johnston (1901: p. 152), and probably many other investigators have confused this Dr. Clark with Darwin's last doctor, Sir Andrew Clark, who was not born until 1826.

found to yield, under the influence of this, to remedies which previously made little or no impression on them.

. . . . .

The daily increasing size of our watering-places, and the deserted state of a great part of London during several months, are sufficient proofs, not to mention others, of the growing conviction that, for the preservation of health, it is necessary to change, from time to time, the relaxing, I may say deteriorating, atmosphere of a large city for the more pure and invigorating air of the country. When the extent of benefit to be derived from this measure is fully estimated, no person whose circumstances permit will neglect to avail himself of it. It is, indeed, the best, if not the only cure, for that destructive malady which may be justly termed *Cachexia Londinensis,* which preys upon the vitals and stamps its hues upon the countenance of almost every permanent resident in this large city.

. . . . .

In a climate naturally humid, like that of Great Britain, it is of the first importance in the selection of a situation for building that it should admit of free circulation of air and thorough drainage. In proportion as the soil is impermeable to, or retentive of humidity, so ought the site of the building to be high, in order to allow of sufficient fall for the water to drain off.

Trees and shrubberies close to houses are not only direct causes of humidity, but they act still more injuriously by impeding a free circulation of air and excluding the sun's rays. This is one of the most frequent, and I may add most powerful causes of insalubrity in country houses in England. . . .

The house at Down fulfilled all of these criteria. It stood on high, generally well-drained land,[3] in the chalk country of the North Downs. There were few trees about and the adjacent valleys were dry throughout the year. The house was tall and, when first occupied by Darwin, nearly devoid of enclosing shrubbery (F. Darwin, 1888: **1:** p. 319). It was far enough away from London so as not to be seriously affected by the city's unhealthy airs, but close enough to it to be reached after a journey of several hours by coach.

[3] After a rain the water would puddle in the clay soil for a few days.

SOME PSYCHIATRIC OPINIONS

THE IMAGE of Darwin in seclusion at Down as a chronically ill individual, sapped of energy and aesthetic sensitivity, wearing a black cloak and hat, and plagued by diverse symptoms of psychogenic origin, has a firm place in the minds of most individuals who know anything about him. Yet he did not look ill—he had an out-of-doors complexion—and the inability of the doctors to diagnose the cause of his ailment led some of his contemporaries to suspect him of being a hypochondriac. This has been reinforced by the writings of psychiatrists and psychologists during the past fifty years. The unusually detailed record of Darwin's life and thoughts as revealed in his correspondence, autobiography, and writings has been a fertile source for the development of post-mortem hypotheses. The first elaborate psychological interpretation was proposed by Edward Kempf in 1920 in his tome, *Psychopathology*. According to his view (1920: p. 250) Darwin's illness was a reflection of an anxiety neurosis relating to his:

. . . complete submission to his father whereby he deprived himself of all channels of self-assertion in his relations with his father or anything that pertained to him. Free assertions for his rights might have led to a mortal father-son conflict, because both had irrepressible affective cravings that contended for the idealization of the same love-object. This would, perhaps, as it so often does, have terminated in Darwin becoming a paranoiac, if not an invalid. His search for the secrets of nature and his mother's love would then have become hopelessly aborted by hate. Through the renunciation of all envy and all competitive interests in life, such as ambition for priority, and the unreserved acceptance of his father's word and wisdom, Darwin, by adroitly selecting diversions, succeeded in keeping suppressed all disconcerting affective reactions with no more inconvenience than that of producing nutritional disturbances, uncomfortable cardiac and vaso-motor reactions, vertigo and insomnia.

This was the beginning of a long line of psychoanalytical reconstructions.[4] Douglas Hubble (1946: pp. 82–83) believed that

4

Darwin's obsessive urge for work and achievement was the product of suppression or non-recognition of the fear, guilt, or hate felt toward his father who had unjustly condemned him for being idle during his youth. Hubble further suggested that Darwin was neither very intelligent nor quick-witted and this was said to have been partly reflected in Darwin's apparent need to ruminate during the night hours and, by implication, in his need to remove himself from distractions by moving from London to Down. Without his psychogenic illness, therefore, he would never have achieved eminence (*ibid.*, p. 85): "To have cured Charles Darwin's illness would have both lessened his ambition and destroyed his way of achievement," and (1943: p. 133): "It is a terrifying thought that the Darwins of today may be known to posterity only in the case-books of the psychiatrists" (see also Hubble, 1953).

The basic theme developed by Kempf and Hubble was elaborated upon by Rankine Good in 1954 (1954a: pp. 106–107). The evidence of Darwin's expressed love toward his father may at first appear to be in conflict with the views of most psychiatrists, but Good (see also Greenacre, 1963: p. 55) resolved the problem to his own satisfaction by stating:

. . . there is a wealth of evidence that unmistakably points to these symptoms as a distorted expression of aggression, hate, and resentment felt, at an unconscious level, by Darwin towards his tyrannical father, although, at a conscious level we find the reaction-formation of the reverence for his father which was boundless and almost touching.

And, along a similar line, ". . . the picture of Darwin as a kindly, tolerant father in an atmosphere of uninterrupted love and affection," presumably as revealed by the letters and memoirs of his

---

4 Kempf also felt that Darwin had strong homosexual tendencies, and that he may have feared going into the ministry for this reason. His argument is rather obscure. Part of it involves the condition of Darwin's hands prior to his departure from England aboard the *Beagle* and his wish to take arsenic as a medicine. When Darwin later mentioned that he might not take the arsenic after all, Kempf believed this indicated that he had properly controlled his sexual interest in Captain FitzRoy: he had ". . . met the emergency and mastered himself completely . . ." (Kempf, 1920: pp. 224–225).

children and friends, was very probably a mask which covered a terrible type of tyranny, the kind that results from the exploitation of a chronic illness. In sum, then, Good believed that even if Darwin ". . . did not slay his father in the flesh, then in his *The Origin of Species* . . . &c, he certainly slew the Heavenly Father in the realm of natural history," and, as in the case of Oedipus, his punishment for the unconscious patricide was almost forty years of severe and crippling neurotic suffering.

Some of the more recent psychologically oriented views on the subject resemble those already mentioned. Ernest Jones (1959: p. 204) believed that both Darwin and Alfred Wallace paid the penalty for having committed unconscious patricide. Darwin suffered "a crippling and lifelong neurosis," and Wallace "compensated for the displacement of the supernatural by bringing it back in another sphere, by his quite naive adherence to spiritistic beliefs." Although this well-known psychoanalyst did not bring up the name of Thomas Huxley in this context, it is possible to find intimations in the more general literature that Huxley also may have been ill during much of his life because of a neurosis arising from an unspecified repression (see Bibby, 1959, p. 12, for example). The psychiatrist Phyllis Greenacre (1963: pp. 33, 58, 60) believes Darwin suffered early from a severe confusion of sexual orientation and that he turned to science because of his ambivalent identification with his father and grandfather, ". . . but even more from reactions to sadomasochistic fantasies concerning his own birth and his mother's death." His symptoms were the result of a severe anxiety neurosis in an obsessional character, and much complicated by genius. This last statement is somewhat similar to one made by Professor A. W. Woodruff (1965: p. 749; 1968: p. 671). Mrs. Darwin's disapproval of some of her husband's work has also been advanced as a possible cause of his chronic illness (Darlington, 1959: pp. 47–48).

In so far as a number of psychologists have readily admitted that the tests their colleagues have constructed over the years have been frequently biased in favor of individuals with values and backgrounds relatively similar to their own (see, for example, Anne Roe, 1953: pp. 50–52; Liam Hudson, 1966: pp. 4, 113; Sir Cyril Burt's introduction to Arthur Koestler, *The Act of Creation*), it seems legitimate to ask whether some psychologists and psychiatrists have not done the same thing they believed Darwin was doing: provided an interpretation of his illness which best served their own sublimated neuroses. The occurrence of such neuroses may well have encouraged some of them to have chosen their profession in the first place. Darwin's father might not have had quite the splendid character which Michael Kelly claims for him (1964: pp. 74–79; see also Barlow, 1954: pp. 414–415), and Darwin's love for his father might have been clouded by ambivalent feelings, but this is one of the commonplaces of human existence and does not satisfactorily explain either his illness, his deep commitment to his life's work, or the source and motivation of his many and varied inspiring insights. The "wealth of evidence" claimed by Good to support his case (to be discussed), and the evidence used by other psychologists and psychiatrists, are frequently derived from the same set of examples. One of the most commonly cited is the statement in Darwin's *Autobiography* (Barlow, 1958: p. 28) regarding his father's opinion of his son's non-academic pursuits: "To my deep mortification my father once said to me, 'You care for nothing but shooting, dogs, and rat-catching, and you will be a disgrace to yourself and all your family.' " According to the standards of the day (if not today, also) this statement was probably quite warranted, for young Charles had not exhibited a disciplined use of his time, a fact which Darwin, himself, came to recognize: "He was very properly vehement against my turning an idle sporting man, which then seemed my probable destination" (*ibid.*, p. 56). Even as late as the age of twenty-two Darwin gave priority to partridge hunting over an opportunity to acquire additional geological knowledge in the field from one of the most eminent geologists in Great Britain, Adam Sedgwick. This was at a time when he knew very little about the subject and yet had decided that geology was to be his primary intellectual interest (*ibid.,* p. 71). Sedgwick, too, must have recognized this characteristic in his young pupil, for he wrote to Darwin's former headmaster at Shrewsbury School when Charles had nearly completed his long voyage in the *Beagle:* "There was some risk of his turning out an idle man, but his character will now be fixed . . ." (Clark and Hughes, 1890: **1:** p. 380). In addition, Darwin's private assessment of his father's words seems to indicate that their harshness was untypical and therefore that much more poignant: "But my father, who was the kindest man I ever knew, and whose memory I love with all my heart, must have been angry and somewhat unjust when he used such words" (Barlow, 1958: p. 28). To convert his relatively private confession of love into the opposite interpretation is easy enough, but unless it is supported by convincing collateral evidence, acceptance depends upon a willingness to submit to the largely intuitive, and often conflicting, opinions of some psychologists (Barlow, 1954: pp. 414–415). Dr. Saul Adler, who developed the idea that Darwin may have suffered from Chagas's disease, made the same type of observation (Kelly, 1967: p. 341): "It is only too easy to cook up a neurosis for any case in which it is difficult to establish a diagnosis and once it is cooked up it can be elaborated *ad lib*" (see also Roberts, 1966: p. 724). An examination of the conclusions of one influential writer on the subject, already cited above, the medical psychologist Rankine Good, will help to illustrate this point.

G OOD (1954a; 1954b) developed in detail the theme of Darwin's supposed revolt against his father. His argument, which uses many examples in common with other psychologically disposed interpretations, is principally based on the following seven points (and the one just discussed):

1. *Darwin's father dominated his household and created a stifling and inhibitory atmosphere for his children.* "*He had the art of making everyone obey him to the letter and the power of producing fear of himself in others . . .*" (Good, 1954*b:* p. 12).[5]

This statement appears to be largely derived from the following passage written by Darwin about his father in his autobiography (Barlow, 1958: pp. 39–40):

Owing to his strong memory he knew an extraordinary number of curious stories, which he liked to tell, as he was a great talker. He was generally in high spirits, and laughed and joked with every one—often with his servants—with the utmost freedom: yet he had the art of making every one obey him to the letter. Many persons were much afraid of him.

After giving two examples of this, and pointing out the unusual empathy he had with the sufferings of other people, he went on to state: "Yet, he was generally in high spirits. He was easily made very angry, but as his kindness was unbounded, he was widely and deeply loved." Darwin also recalled his father's very generous and sympathetic character: "His sympathy was not only

---

[5] It is interesting to note that *all* of the eight creative scientists (physical and biological) examined by the psychiatrist Peter L. Giovacchini, were reported to have had ". . . extremely domineering mothers who ruled the household by their aggressiveness. . . . The patients' fathers, on the other hand, were described as mild, submissive, passive men whose role in the family was a subordinate one and, in some cases, an inferior and depreciated one. All the patients manifested considerable hostility to them . . ." (Giovacchini, 1960: pp. 415–416). On the other hand, another view is that the creative scientists tend to have been raised by affectionate and permissive parents (see, for example, Getzels and Csikszentmihalyi, 1967: p. 84).

9

with the distresses of others, but in a greater degree with the pleasure of all around him." When Charles revealed a pronounced tendency to tell fibs as a young boy, his father chose to make light of them, rather than treat them as a crime. He was also liberal in other ways, such as being very willing to confide in Charles about the details of his work, and to give him a share of responsibility for taking care of some of his patients when the boy was but sixteen years of age (*ibid.*, pp. 23, 29, 47). When Charles and his brother showed an interest in chemistry their father built a little laboratory for them and bought equipment for it (Darwin Papers, no. 112, 1882). The Reverend William Leighton, a friend of Charles at primary school, remembered that he preferred to run home rather than join in play with the other boys (Darwin Papers, no. 112, 1882?), and when he transferred to Dr. Butler's boarding school he very often took advantage of the free periods to spend the time with his family, which, he wrote, ". . . was in many ways advantageous to me by keeping up home affections and interests" (Barlow, 1958: p. 25; see also George Darwin, in Darwin Papers, no. 112, 1882).

The implication that Charles abjectly acquiesced to all of his father's expressed wishes is not borne out by the evidence available. The only known specific complaint Robert Darwin had regarding his younger son was that he was too preoccupied with ". . . shooting, dogs, and rat-catching. . .," an appraisal that was not too far from the truth, and yet young Charles continued to hunt and collect objects of natural history with undiminished fervor.

It would seem, therefore, that Good's depiction of the Darwin household at Shrewsbury was not entirely a balanced one. There were undoubtedly many moments when Robert Darwin asserted his strong personality, but there were also periods when his high spirits and laughter must have created a happy atmosphere at "The Mount." He was not a cold Victorian father-figure. He had a sympathetic personality, was concerned about the welfare of the poor in his community, held no dogmatic religious beliefs (he was a skeptic), and he shared many of his experiences with his son. In 1849, a few months after his father's death, Charles wrote to his friend J. D. Hooker: "On the 13th of November, my poor father died, and no one who did not know him would believe that a man above eighty-three years old could have retained so tender and affectionate a disposition" (F. Darwin, 1888: **1**: p. 372).

2. *"As well as sharing with the rest of the family this stifling and inhibitory atmosphere, Darwin had personal reason enough to feel resentment and antagonism toward his father. The latter, for instance, had, since Darwin was doing no good at school, taken him away from it when he was sixteen years old and sent him to Edinburgh to study medicine, although Darwin had never expressed any desire to become a physician"* (Good, 1954b: p. 12).

How Good arrived at this conclusion is not clear. There appears to be nothing in Darwin's autobiography or letters which reveals that he either disliked or in any way attempted to resist his father's decision to send him to Edinburgh. During the summer before his matriculation as a student at the university he assisted his father in his medical practice. According to his autobiography, he ". . . felt a keen interest in the work . . ." and, according to his son Francis, was quite proud of some of his accomplishments. His father freely discussed the ailments of his patients with him and it is clear young Charles took considerable interest in these conversations. Darwin's older brother, Erasmus, to whom he had been quite close, was transferring to Edinburgh as a medical student at the same time. Further indications of Charles's interest in the subject prior to his arrival at Edinburgh is demonstrated by the statement that he could not understand why his interest lapsed after he attended the medical courses at Edinburgh. In retrospect, he remarked that his father's decision to remove him from Shrewsbury School and send him to Edinburgh at the early age of sixteen had been a wise one (Barlow, pp. 36, 46–47).

3. *Another illustration of Robert Darwin's oppressive character was revealed in his opposition to the plan of his son to become the naturalist to the* Beagle. *"Darwin would never have gone on the voyage had it not been for the intervention of an uncle"* (Good, 1954*b:* p. 12).

In view of what we know today, this is an unsettling thought, placing his father in the position of one who would have denied one of the world's greatest scientists the chance to have contributed his ideas to the pool of human knowledge. This type of hindsight has little value in helping to clarify the question of Robert Darwin's influence on his son's development. Even today it is considered remarkable and largely inexplicable that this rather ordinary young man—in terms of conventional interpretation—was able to have made anything but the most prosaic contributions from his geographical experiences (see especially de Beer, 1968: pp. 68–71). The initial objections raised by Robert Darwin were stated by his son in a letter to his former professor, J. S. Henslow (F. Darwin, 1888: **1**: p. 195): "My father's objections are these:

. . . the unfitting me to settle down as a Clergyman, my little habit of seafaring,[6] *the shortness of time,* and the chance of my not suiting Captain Fitz-Roy. It is certainly a very serious objection, the very short time for all my preparations, as not only body but mind wants making up for such an undertaking.

To this were added some other objections—the accommodations would be most uncomfortable, it would constitute another (a third) change in Charles's professional objectives, and the desirability of the position was suspect, probably having been offered to others and turned down by them. Another objection was brought

6 Robert Darwin may have suspected that his son was prone to nausea and seasickness (a point to be discussed). Later, on learning of an act of kindness by Captain FitzRoy when his son was suffering badly from seasickness, tears were said to have come to his eyes (in F. Darwin, 1888: **1**: p. 332).

out in a letter written by Charles to his father just prior to receiving the latter's permission to go on the voyage. In the letter he attempted to dispel what appears to have been one of his father's primary concerns: "The danger appears to me and all the Wedgwoods not great . . ." (Barlow, 1945: p. 25).

Most of the points raised by Robert Darwin appear to be reasonable when placed against the rather uncertain character of his son's interests and accomplishments as a student. In addition, Charles had developed his own doubts before his father's approval was given (Barlow, 1933: p. 3):

I shall never forget what very anxious and uncomfortable days these two were, my heart appeared to sink within me, independently of the doubts raised by my Father's dislike to the scheme. I could scarcely make up my mind to leave England even for the time which I then thought the voyage would last. Lucky indeed it was for me that the first picture of the expedition was such a highly coloured one.

This was underscored in one of Darwin's first letters to his father during the course of the expedition (F. Darwin, 1888: 1: p. 332):

. . . I am now more fully aware of your wisdom in throwing cold water on the whole scheme; the chances are so numerous of [it] turning out quite the reverse; to such an extent do I feel this, that if my advice was asked by any person on a similar occasion, I should be very cautious in encouraging him.

That Robert Darwin was not inflexible may be seen by the fact that Charles's maternal uncle, Josiah Wedgwood, helped to persuade him to change his mind. The thought that the uncle may represent the enlightened and liberal thinker while the father represents the unreasonable authoritarian figure gains little support from this episode. It is quite clear that Robert had some reasonable objections to the plan. The social role of the maternal uncle is quite different from that of the father in most cultures, including that of Western Europe, and this may well be accentuated when the uncle's sister has died, as had Mrs. Robert Darwin.

4. *Darwin's conscious high regard for his father was, in fact, a "... 'reaction-formation' against the undoubted deeper un-*

conscious feelings of aggression and resentment against the tyrannical figure of his father." Some of the clues to these deeper unconscious feelings are revealed in the manner in which he referred to his father in correspondence written while he was traveling around the world. Thus, he spelled the first letter of "father" with a capital; in two letters not addressed to him he added his love to his father in some post-scripts, and in another letter, addressed to one of his sisters, he wrote: "My dear Caroline, I do long to see you and all the rest of you [i.e. his other sisters and his brother] & my dear Father"; in one letter to his father he discovered after the first page he had been writing to his sisters instead! (Good, 1954b: p. 13).

Some of the more general aspects of this point were discussed earlier; only the specific items will now be discussed. Capitalization of the first letter of "father" for one's parent was a common practice at that time. Darwin alternated between using the upper and lower case in his various writings, and he used the upper case when referring to the fathers of other individuals (see, for example, Darwin, in Barlow, 1945: p. 120). When writing to his own children about his wife he spoke of her as "your Mother" (Barlow, 1958: p. 96), and he also capitalized "brother" (*ibid.,* pp. 48, 87). His son, Francis, also sometimes capitalized the first letter of "father" (see, for example, F. Darwin, in Barlow, 1958: p. 23), and a number of Darwin's contemporaries did the same thing. The Reverend W. A. Leighton, his school friend, capital-ized the first letters of both "mother" and "father" in a letter addressed to Francis Darwin, and written in about 1882 (Darwin Papers, no. 112, 1882?), and Justice John M. Herbert, another of Darwin's early friends, used the upper case for "father" in a similar letter sent to Francis Darwin (*ibid.,* 1882).

The second item concerned the inclusion of remembrances to his father in letters written to other members of the family. This would seem to require little comment. Good's view that this placed Darwin's father apart from the rest of the family is possibly correct, but it does not necessarily follow that there are ominous undertones connected with this, any more than with the capitalized first letter of "father." The simple fact is that Robert Darwin *was* the father, both from the standpoint of genealogy and role. If he had not stood apart from his sons and daughters he probably would have been liable to other unflattering interpretations.

The last item, the fact that Darwin began (and ended) a letter to his father, although part of the way through he discovered he had been writing to his sisters instead, may have a less complex reason than that raised by Good. The letter in question was begun on February 8 or 9, 1832 (Darwin admitted to being confused as to his dates), and was added to on February 26 and March 1. When he began the letter he was one day's sail past St. Jago in the Cape Verde Islands and was suffering from a mild case of seasickness. The entry in his diary for that day consisted of only one sentence, stating that although the day was calm and beautiful, he was unable to enjoy it because he felt ". . . squeamish & uncomfortable. . . ." A prolonged period of nausea without the relief of vomiting is not conducive to either letter writing or to good concentration. The following day—the second day's sail past St. Jago—the *Beagle* came in sight of a British ship. Darwin took advantage of the opportunity by writing a second letter to his father and sending it by this ship; the first letter was sent later from Brazil (Barlow, 1933: p. 34; Barlow, 1945: pp. 52–59).

5. *Darwin makes no reference to his father's views on evolution. If Robert Darwin had been favorably disposed toward the concept his son would certainly have mentioned it, and Charles ". . . would not have carried such a heavy-laden complement of guilt-feeling." Further, ". . . the revolutionary usually rests content with murdering the cherished beliefs of his father and for a variable time thereafter suffers conscious remorse. Darwin, however, did more than settle a purely personal*

quarrel, for if he did not slay his Father in the flesh, then, certainly, . . . he forced his quarrel on the rest of humanity by slaying the Heavenly Father in the realm of natural history" (Good, 1954*b:* pp. 11–12, 15).

That Darwin failed to mention whether or not his father knew or approved of his theory of evolution is negative evidence of questionable significance. At the time Darwin was developing the theory he and his father lived some distance apart, and his father died some eleven years before the publication of *The Origin of Species.* Nor is there information about the opinion Robert had of his son's popular *Journal of Researches,* his coral-reef theory, his theory regarding the origin of the Parallel Roads of Glenroy, or any other of his important contributions up to that time. Darwin's recollection about his father almost exclusively dealt with his character and mental attributes as an individual and a physician. His father did not appear to have an interest in natural history and, according to Charles, his ". . . mind was not scientific, and he did not generalise his knowledge under general laws . . . ," although this did not stop him from forming intuitive opinions on a wide range of subjects (Barlow, 1958: p. 42). His son also described him as being ". . . not very studious or mentally receptive, except for facts in conversation—great collector of anecdotes . . ." (F. Darwin, 1888: **3:** p. 179). Consequently, there was probably little basis for a scientific exchange between the two men and there would have been little reason for Charles to have recorded his father's opinion on the subject.

Robert Darwin was a confirmed agnostic or atheist (Barlow, 1958: p. 87, 96; F. Darwin, 1888: **3:** p. 179). Even if it could be demonstrated that he had disagreed with his son's conclusions, their differences would have been on an intellectual rather than a moral or religious basis. Robert's own father, Erasmus, had been a skeptic and an early evolutionist. The statement by Good that Charles Darwin had murdered the cherished beliefs of his father is simply incorrect. If he slew the Heavenly Father as a substitute for his own father, then he went to a great deal of trouble for nothing.

6. *Darwin's feeling of guilt was also revealed in a statement once made by him that to mention his belief that species were not immutable was ". . . like confessing a murder. . . ." And, according to Good, ". . . from a psychological point of view, . . . when Darwin stated that it was* like confessing a murder, *he was indubitably stating that it* was *a murder." Good justified his position by stating: ". . . a study of the development of the semantic sense in children, or the study of the same development in foreigners learning a language, or the psychological associations of patients afflicted with psychological disorder shows plainly that metaphor precedes simile in the calendar of semantic development; that identification, as established by metaphor, is a normal primitive mode of expression (and archaic modes of expression are characteristic of unconscious mental functioning) before the reality sense becomes sufficiently developed to make a part identification or comparison"* (Good, 1954b: p. 11).

The oft-quoted "like confessing a murder" phrase is taken from a letter written by Darwin to J. D. Hooker before they had become well acquainted. In the letter Darwin exposed his vulnerable side by discussing his hypothesis about the origin of species, and he was clearly apprehensive over what Hooker's reaction might be. He had spoken of his idea to few other scientists:

. . . I have been now ever since my return engaged in a very presumptuous work, and I know no one individual who would not say a very foolish one. . . At last gleams of light have come, and I am almost convinced (quite contrary to the opinion I started with) that species are not (it is like confessing a murder) immutable. . . . I think I have found out (here's presumption!) the simple way by which species become exquisitely adapted to various ends. You will now groan, and think to yourself, "on what a man have I been wasting my time and writing to." I should, five years ago, have thought so [too]. . . (F. Darwin, 1888: 2: pp. 23–24; also F. Darwin and Seward, 1903: 1: pp. 40–41).

When taken in its context the phrase has a quite different ring. Darwin fully realized the disruptive implications of his idea and he was making sure that Hooker knew this. The assertion that Darwin was reverting to a primitive stage of semantic development, when he wrote the phrase, can at best be described as imaginative.

7. *The proposition that ". . . it was actually a murder in his unconscious mind can be confirmed in various ways. To take a single instance, a murder in unconscious mental functioning demands the death of the murderer in expiation—and we find Darwin's quite irrational expectation of sudden death when he was thirty-five years old and his leaving, as his solemn last request, instructions about what had to be done with the sketch of his species theory." The guilt Good believed Darwin to have suffered from was expressed ". . . at the terrible cost of almost forty years of severe and crippling neurotic suffering . . ." (Good, 1954b: pp. 11, 16).*

On July 5, 1844, at the age of thirty-five, Darwin wrote in his personal journal: "Sent a written Sketch of Species theory (seven years after commencement) in about 230 pages to Mr. Fletcher to be copied. . ." (de Beer, 1959: p. 11). That same day he wrote instructions to his wife regarding whom to contact to edit and act as his agent in locating a publisher for his manuscript ". . . in case of sudden death. . . ." He also stated: "If, as I believe, my theory in time be accepted even by one competent judge, it will be a considerable step in science." The time and labor expended in developing the theory, his realization of its profound significance, and his general deep concern over the preservation of all of his notes and books (F. Darwin, 1888: **1**: p. 152), were sufficient reasons for him to want to ensure its survival in the event of his death. Ten years later he added an amendment to these instructions on the back of the same letter (*ibid.* **2**: pp. 16–18).

To refer to these instructions as an ". . . irrational expectation

of sudden death . . . ," and an unconscious expression of the
desire to murder himself, is one more demonstration of the ex-
cesses of this interpretation and others like it. Prior to this time
Darwin had been very ill with symptoms that included violent
heart palpitations. He suspected he had heart disease. In 1841
his father told him he would not become strong for some years
(*ibid.* 1: p. 272) and this prognosis was correct. Obviously,
during a prolonged fatal illness, Darwin would have had the
opportunity to express his wishes to those he had decided should
edit and publish his manuscript. It was only in case of sudden
death, such as a heart attack, that the instructions to his wife had
any meaning. As in previous examples, there is no basis to justify
a deeper reading of the significance of the phrase.

The absence of detailed criticism of studies like those written
by Rankine Good, Douglas Hubble, and Edward Kempf permitted
the idea of Darwin as a deeply disturbed and psychosomatically
ill individual to gain a firm place in present-day thinking. It
underlies a number of recent serious and semi-popular works on
Darwin, and even those who do not seem readily predisposed to
accept the psychiatrists' interpretation often accept the view that
he was a hypochondriac. To this question the discussion now turns.

THE QUESTION OF HYPOCHONDRIA

THE PRIMARY LINE of direct evidence used to support the claim that Darwin was a hypochondriac is based on the existence of a diary in which Darwin kept a day-to-day record of his ailments, how he felt, and what cures he had tried (i.e. douche, shallow bath, etc.), and other notes of similar content. Professor A. W. Woodruff (1968: p. 671), W. D. Foster (1965: p. 478), Sir Peter Medawar (1967: p. 67), and others have favored the idea that such detailed attention reveals the obsessional nature of his illness. Sir Peter has suggested that an initial physical origin may have been partly obscured by the neurotic element of his illness:

> Ill people suspected of hypochondria or malingering have to pretend to be iller than they really are and may then get taken in by their own deception. They do this to convince others, but Darwin had also to convince himself, for he had no privileged insight into what was wrong with him. The entries in Darwin's notebooks that bear on his health read to me like the writings of a man desperately reassuring himself of the reality of his illness. "There," one can imagine his saying, "I *am* ill, I must be ill; for how otherwise could I feel like this?"

As a general statement Medawar's point is probably valid. It is difficult to conceive of any prolonged organic illness that would not affect an individual's emotional equilibrium in some way, and in certain cases the illness might be seriously reinforced for the social and personal reasons outlined by Sir Peter. The problem is, of course, not whether such situations exist, but whether or not there is sufficient evidence available to develop a case for the primarily or partially hypochondriacal genesis of Darwin's illness. It is rather easy to make a vague comparison between the habits of "typical" individuals plagued by chronic illness, and those of Darwin, but this can only be done by ignoring his unique character and background. His father was a practicing physician, his brother obtained a degree in medicine, and Darwin himself spent two

20

years as a medical student at Edinburgh and believed he possessed
". . . a smattering of medical knowledge;" when during the summer before attending the University of Edinburgh he helped his
father treat some poor patients in Shrewsbury:

> . . . I wrote down as full an account as I could of the cases with all the
> symptoms, and read them aloud to my father, who suggested further en-
> quiries, and advised what medicines to give, which I made up myself.
> At one time I had at least a dozen patients, and I felt a keen interest in the
> work.

His son, Francis, recalled that he had been quite proud of the
successful treatment of an entire family (Barlow, 1958: pp. 47,
79). It is also apparent from the shopping lists Darwin compiled
during the voyage of the *Beagle* that he was accustomed to buying
medicines which he presumably administered to himself (to be
discussed). As a scientist he excelled in providing solutions for
difficult problems over a wide range of subjects. He had learned
the value of exhaustively collecting any facts that might have a
bearing on the problem that concerned him, and few problems
concerned him more than the bad state of his health. It would
be surprising, therefore, if he had not compiled a detailed record of
his illness. In 1854, at approximately the same time he was
making observations in his health diary, he wrote to his friend,
J. D. Hooker (F. Darwin and Seward, 1903: **1**: p. 78):

> I am really truly sorry to hear about your [poor health]. I entreat you to
> write down your own case,—symptoms, and habits of life,—and then
> consider your case as that of a stranger. . . .[7]

Considering the state of internal medicine at the time, the inability of doctors to cure his malady, and the character, habits, and

---

[7] Darwin tended to approach many problems in the same way. Earlier, when he
was debating whether or not he should get married he carefully listed all of the
pro and con arguments (see Barlow, 1958: pp. 231–234). He also kept a record
of the day he started on a holiday and the day he returned, and for many years he
systematically kept the score of the backgammon games he and his wife had played;
in a similar manner he carefully recorded an annotated list of the pieces of music
his wife had played which he had especially appreciated (F. Darwin, 1888: **1**:
pp. 123–124, 129).

scientific background of Darwin, this was an expression of common sense, and not the recommendation of a hypochondriac.

The statement by his son, Francis, about his father's chronic ill health also has an important bearing on this question. As the editor of his father's correspondence, diary, and other personal materials, Francis became aware for the first time of the full extent of his father's suffering (F. Darwin, 1888: **1**: p. 159):

> He bore his illness with such uncomplaining patience, that even his children can hardly, I believe, realise the extent of his habitual suffering. In their case the difficulty is heightened by the fact that, from the days of their earliest recollections, they saw him in constant ill-health,—and saw him, in spite of it, full of pleasure in what pleased them. Thus, in later life, their perception of what he endured had to be disentangled from the impression produced in childhood by constant genial kindness under conditions of unrecognized difficulty. No one indeed, except my mother, knows the full amount of suffering he endured, or the full amount of his wonderful patience.

This, too, is not the picture of an individual who was attempting to exploit his illness, unconsciously or consciously, real or imagined.[8]

Lawrence A. Kohn, in a review of the problem of Darwin's illness, expressed doubts about the hypochondria hypothesis for another reason (1963: p. 240):

> It is surprising that there is [almost] nowhere mention of medication. Most of the treatment of the time seems to us incredibly naive, but doctors dosed freely. What did Darwin take when he was exhausted, when he had indigestion? Hypochondriacs as a rule like to talk about such things yet nowhere in the records do we find: "Dr. so-and-so gave me this or that, but I worsened on it, and stopped taking the nauseous mixture." Possibly at Down House, which is now the property of the Royal College of Surgeons, more might be learned, but from the published accounts we do not know if he even took bicarbonate of soda. . . .

The records at Down House do not appear to provide additional information on this subject, although they have never been pub-

---

[8] Darwin's father, who pronounced Darwin's professor of geology, Adam Sedgwick, a confirmed hypochondriac after their first meeting (Clark and Hughes, 1890: **1**: p. 380), apparently did not believe his son suffered from this same disability, for he told his son in 1841 that he did not expect him to become strong for a number of years (F. Darwin, 1888: **1**: p. 272).

lished in full (Foster, 1965). Based upon his reading of Darwin's letters and the testimony of his relatives and friends, Kohn went on to make the point that throughout his years of illness Darwin revealed the kind of emotional maturity which does not fit the pattern of the neurotic (1963: p. 250). Darwin was capable of mature love, the responsibilities of fatherhood, long-lasting friendships, and was generous with his time and money:

He was truly large in spirit, and if he chose to voice his suffering rather than endure it in silence; if he benefited indirectly from suggestive psychotherapy as have patients with many forms of organic disease, this alone does not prove that he was neurotically ill.

After having spent many hours reading published and unpublished personal correspondence by, or about, Darwin, the present writer came to the same conclusion. It was, in fact, for this reason that he became skeptical about the psychological interpretations and began to investigate this subject.

Other reasons have been advanced to support the psychologically oriented diagnosis. Like those already discussed, their value depends largely upon the reader's preconceptions. With the principal exception of Sir Peter Medawar, who suggests both a pathological and psychological cause, and Professor A. W. Woodruff, the various works do not attempt to investigate the possibility of an organic origin for Darwin's illness before developing their themes on Darwin's neuroses. Inability to identify an organic disease which fits all or most of Darwin's symptoms and the course of development of his illness is one of the reasons for this neglect.

VICTORIAN DYSPEPSIA AND ITS AUTHORS

D ARWIN'S symptoms are numerous and diverse, but they do fit an obvious pattern. A great many of them fit into what Darwin's doctor, presumably James Clark, referred to as "dyspepsia," which was apparently one of the more common serious disease syndromes recognized by English doctors during the middle part of the last century. Clark, it will be remembered, was probably one of two doctors consulted by Darwin immediately after his return home from the voyage of the *Beagle*. He was a baronet, a Fellow of the Royal Society, physician to the Duchess of Kent, and physician-in-ordinary to Queen Victoria. He was also a friend and walking companion of Charles Lyell (Lyell, 1881: **2**: pp. 157–158, 327, 368–369, 371). In 1946 T. G. Wilson described him in the following terms (1946: pp. 93, 94):

> Clark has been portrayed as a futile, doddering old Court physician, trusted implicitly by the Queen, and refusing aid from his fellow-doctors. Nevertheless, he was no fool, as his record shows. He made no addition to medical knowledge, but he was an accomplished "medical politician," like so many fashionable London physicians of later days.

> . . . . .

> He cannot be called a failure, for he made full use of the talents which had been given him. His writings make it quite clear that his greatest disability was a lack of brains, for which he cannot be blamed. In his early days, Sir James had made his name in much the same way as Wilde, by publishing an account of the climate, diseases, and medical schools of the countries he visited as a medical attendant to [one of] his patient[s].

Whether or not this assessment partly reflects the prejudice of applying present-day standards to the past, it would still seem that Clark may not have been the type of physician best suited to diagnose a complicated ailment.

One type of dyspepsia described by Clark which involved a number of the symptoms exhibited by Darwin was known as "nervous dyspepsia." Such patients usually had a variable appetite, were flatulent, commonly suffered from diarrhea although sometimes from constipation, did not sleep well and awoke unrefreshed, commonly had headaches, and especially bad ones upon waking, and had "strong mental impressions." The air of crowded rooms often precipitated these symptoms. Headaches were at times sudden, usually preceded by a sense of coldness and creeping on the surface, which was thought to account for the frequent shivering. Sometimes attacks were preceded by numbness in the extremities, by dimness of vision or other ocular symptoms; in other patients a peculiar uneasy sensation was experienced, originating in one of the extremities and gradually ascending to the head, "resembling the aura epileptica." Nausea or vomiting also occurred among some of the nervous dyspeptics. The gastric complaints were sometimes intense and at other times scarcely noticeable (J. Clark, 1846: p. 17–19).

Another recognized form of this disease was "atonic dyspepsia." Patients possessed little or no appetite, often had a loathing for food, and sometimes had bouts of nausea. Vomiting, headaches, vertigo, faintness, cramps, clammy perspiration, epigastric pain, great distension and fetid eructations were common. These types of dyspepsia sometimes merged into each other (*ibid.,* pp. 15–17).

Additional insight into the talents of Dr. Clark may be detected in his discussion about digestive problems (*ibid.,* p. 20):

We also find that the morbid state of the digestive organs extends its influence to other systems; giving rise to various affections of the skin, of the joints, and of the nervous system. Among the last may be mentioned, in addition to headaches, convulsive affections, tic douloureux, paralysis, amaurosis, deafness, loss of smell, loss of voice, spasmodic cough, asthma, palpitation, &c.

Hypochondria and dyspepsia were believed to be closely related (*ibid.,* p. 33):

I class the hypochondriac with the dyspeptic patients, because, without venturing to affirm that hypochondriasis always originates in dyspepsia, I think it may be safely asserted that the former is very rarely met with unaccompanied by more or less of the latter, and in a large proportion of the cases both acknowledge the same origin and are cured by the same means.

Clark does not mention the kinds of medicine he gave to his patients. His primary interest in writing the book was to recommend diets, baths, and a change of scenery and residence. Elsewhere we learn that he sometimes dosed his patients with calomel, and was accused by Prince Albert of poisoning the Princess Royal with this concoction (Longford, 1964: p. 160).

A contemporary of Dr. Clark, and also a prominent physician in London, was Henry Hunt, a specialist in neuralgic disorders. Like most of his colleagues he believed in the value of cold baths, rub-downs, diets, purges, bloodletting, and strong, potentially toxic, medicines. Liquor potassae arsenitis, or Fowler's solution, and the mercury preparation, calomel, were considered to be useful in curing many disorders. The history of one of his patients being treated for tic douloureux arising from dyspepsia provides one more glimpse into the medication of the time (1844: pp. 29–33):

The tone of his stomach was very seriously injured, and unequivocal symptoms of indigestion, and among them the presence of acid, were the result. . . .

After an emetic and aperient draught of rhubarb and sulphate of potash, warmed with sal volatile, I gave him the following draught three times a day, an hour before his meals:

. . . .Liq. Arsenicalis . . .
. . . .Camph. comp. . . .
Aquae cinnam. . . .
M. ft. haustus.

increasing the quantity of liquor arsenicalis daily, until he felt its action on the stomach, which he did, when each dose amounted to twelve minims: it was then discontinued. As soon as he perceived the effect of the medicine, the violent plunges of pain diminished, slowly but regularly, until at the expiration of a fortnight they had altogether ceased. By this time, the action of the arsenic had also subsided; he again took it in doses of five minims, and continued it until all tenderness and pain of the cheek was entirely overcome. This was effected at the expiration of a month from the time of my first seeing him. He then left my neighbourhood, with directions to take the medicine for some months, occasionally omitting it for a fortnight or three weeks, increasing gradually the interval, and decreasing the period, in which he took it.

The patient later wrote that he did not believe he was entirely cured because of a sensation of numbness and tingling he was then feeling which he had formerly regarded as a precursor of an attack.

Hunt believed that medicines such as arsenic should be used well beyond the time the symptoms had disappeared (*ibid.*, p. 37):

One great error, against which patients must be strictly guarded, is the belief of their being cured as soon as the pain is relieved; for unless they patiently persist in taking these remedies, and in following a proper plan of diet until their stomach is quite restored, they will have the mortification and misery of finding, sooner or later, that the pain will return.

Arsenic was also prescribed for intermittent or periodical headaches much as aspirin is today. The recommended plan was to commence with a small quantity and to increase the dose daily until the pain is subdued, ". . . which will seldom be the case until some of the effect of the arsenic on the stomach has been felt. The pain will then be found, almost invariably, to subside," although after the expiration of a week the administration of arsenic should be continued for a few days (*ibid.*, pp. 122, 127, 176). Arsenic combined with calomel was useful as a purge. Neuralgia arising from malaria, and most other cases of neuralgia in which there are distinct and regular intermissions of pain, were most effectively treated by arsenic (*ibid.*, pp. 174–175). Problems resulting from improper functioning of the uterus, from a morbid sensibility of the stomach and intestines, and certain other ailments were treated in the same manner (*ibid.*, pp. 84, 175). If a person became ill after taking arsenic, with, for example, slight nausea and a sinking feeling in the stomach, tingling in the fingers and toes, a flow of warmth all over, and disinclination for food, this should not be viewed with alarm. It is a sign that the medicine is working and the treatment should be discontinued for a period of time (*ibid.*, pp. 91, 177). In addition to all these specific uses of arsenic, it was considered to be an excellent health tonic, and to give firmness and vigor to the constitution, especially for people who are of ". . . lax fibre, accompanied by a languid state of the circulation, and whose secretions are rather profuse than otherwise" (*ibid.,* pp. 173–175).

The numbness and tingling which Hunt's patient with tic douloureux felt is now known to be characteristic of the peripheral neuritis which frequently develops after the administration of arsenic for an extended period of time (C. K. Simpson, 1964: p. 276, for example). In fact, there is little reason to doubt that some of Hunt's patients were victims of this form of medication. One of them, for example, exhibited many of the classic symptoms of fairly advanced chronic arsenicalism: he had conjunctivitis, a catarrhal condition, sensations in his head, attacks of dyspnea (shortness of breath), a "tendency to take cold on least exposure," had difficulty walking uphill, was unusually susceptible to colds, which became increasingly more frequent, suffered from severe indigestion, and his tongue was swollen and furred. Hunt put him on a ". . . course of mild mercurials and saline aperients" (Hunt, 1854: pp. 89–91; for a reference which covers most of the above-listed symptoms in relation to chronic arsenic intoxication, see Buchanan, 1962: pp. 18–19; such symptoms will be discussed more fully later). In an earlier publication by the same physician he stated that the mercurial purges were most useful when mixed with arsenic (Hunt, 1844: p. 176); it is possible therefore that the treatment of this probable case of chronic arsenic intoxication actually included arsenic. Had the patient exhibited some of the other symptoms of this form of chronic poisoning, such as various skin disorders or headaches, it would have been consistent with the practices of the time to have administered arsenic for these also.

Sir Henry Holland has already been mentioned as having been one of Darwin's physicians in 1840 during his residence in London, and he was also consulted as late as 1861 for Darwin's daughter who was seriously ill. He was Charles's brother's physician in 1859 and probably before that time (F. Darwin, 1888: **2:** p. 233; F. Darwin and Seward, 1903: **1:** p. 361). It is also possible that he was consulted during Darwin's years as a student at Cambridge. In February of 1829 young Charles mentioned having spent a day "with Holland" (F. Darwin, 1888: 1: p. 175), and this was one month prior to his being ill for several days with a disorder that periodically reappeared during subsequent years (to be discussed later). Like Sir James Clark, Holland believed in the benefits of moving to "healthful" climates and was concerned with the relationship between the occurrence and morbidity of disease and the temperature, humidity, and electrical state of the atmosphere. James Clark's book was recommended as the best work on the subject (Holland, 1840: pp. 352, 458, 463). Bleeding, especially at the nape of the neck, purgation and strong, potentially toxic, medicines were recommended for certain disorders. One case, that of a man of about fifty-two years of age, may illustrate his type of treatment. The man had suffered for some years from irregular action of the heart, severe gout, severe convulsive twitching of the muscles on one side of his neck, and occasional headaches. Both Holland and Sir Benjamin Brodie treated the case (*ibid.*, p. 345):

. . . the treatment pursued being that of periodical small cuppings on the nape of the neck, bichloride of mercury and morphia; and, at a later time, the sulphate of copper, persisted in for a long period. The same affection recurred, however, about six months after; equally without obvious cause as at first, and scarcely less severe in its degree. In this instance it was seemingly mitigated by cupping, calomel, and a perseverance for sometime in the use of colchicum, though never wholly removed.

Holland recommended the use of colchicum for all chronic forms of gout, for gouty inflammation of the joints, for certain types of headaches, for "gouty bronchitis," and in cases of hypochondriasis, and it was believed usually most effective when combined with calomel (*ibid.*, pp. 145, 149, 151). Today it is recognized that colchicum is very slowly excreted from the body and, ". . . for this reason even small doses repeated in short intervals may lead to severe and fatal poisoning . . ."; the symptoms of this form of poisoning are fairly numerous—one of them is the occurrence of tremors and twitchings of single muscle groups (von Oettingen, 1958: p. 310). According to Holland, if colchicum is given in excess it may do some damage but this is one of the penalties of many effective remedies (1840: p. 153):

> It cannot, from analogy, be thus efficient for good, without the power of inflicting ill; and in the nature of its alkaline ingredient. . . we have an explanation of its general sedative effects, as well as of the more immediate disorder of the stomach following large doses of the medicine. . . .
>
> The proofs of injury, indeed, from wrong or excessive use, even if much more numerous than they are [thought to be], ought not to affect its character as a remedy. The case is common to all other powerful agents of medicine; and further experience will teach us how to obviate these evils, and to correct any which may be inseparable from its use.

Dr. Holland also favored the use of calomel for a wide range of disorders. He believed the dread of this form of mercurial medication in France and Germany was unjustified (*ibid.*, p. 254–264). The use of other purgatives with strong toxic properties, such as gamboge and colocynth, was recommended to combat disease and fever, and he emphasized the importance of giving large doses, which would produce actions different in kind, as well as degree, from those of small doses repeated daily (*ibid.*, p. 111, 113). It is not certain whether his belief in the efficacy of strong alkaline medicines extended to arsenic. In any case, strong alkaline medicines were preferred by him for a very large number of disorders.

Sir Benjamin Brodie, who became president of the Royal Society, and was probably a friend of at least two of Darwin's doctors, Henry Holland and Henry Bence Jones (for a discussion of his possible friendship with Bence Jones see Rosenbloom, 1919; Moreton, 1921), may also have been one of Darwin's physicians.[9] Among his remedies for various ailments may be listed blood-letting over various parts of the body, the use of leeches, blistering,

---

[9] The statement cannot be documented. I believe some time ago I came across a statement to that effect, but because it then held no significance for me, I failed to note the source. In any case, whether this is true or not, Sir Benjamin Brodie may be used as one more representative of the general type of doctor patronized by Darwin during his youth and middle age.

dieting, the administration of opium, arsenic, and the extensive use of mercurial preparations which were given internally, by fumigation, or by a method somewhat resembling acupuncture. Unlike his co-worker, Henry Holland, he believed in the benefits derived from prolonged doses of mercury (Hawkins, 1865: **3**: pp. 297–298):

I have spoken of the necessity of administering mercury, not only till the symptoms are relieved, but for a considerable time afterwards. But you may ask, whether a long course of mercury be not more likely to injure the constitution than a short one? Undoubtedly it is; and that is the very reason why you should prefer a long course. If the course be a short one, the disease is sure to return; you have then to repeat it, and again the disease reappears. Thus you have repeated courses; and not only is the system weakened by the mercury, but the disease, whenever it does return, assumes a more formidable character than before. But if, on the other hand, you put the patient through a long course in the first instance, such a frequent recurrence to the use of mercury will be unnecessary.

Quinine and arsenic were prescribed by him for nervous pains subject to regular intermissions, like those of ague or intermitting fever. When pains occurred daily, or on alternate days, he believed they would always be relieved by combining sulphate of quinine with arsenic, but warned that large doses were sometimes required (*ibid.,* pp. 144, 151). The external administration of nitric acid and arsenic was recommended to destroy warts and tumors. He cautioned his readers, however, that arsenic may have harmful effects (*ibid.,* pp. 151, 360):

. . . I do not know any medicine capable of doing great good, that may not, under certain circumstances, operate as a poison. I saw a gentleman very nearly killed by an over-dose of quinine; others have died in consequence of the imprudent exhibition of the iodide of potassium; and others have been killed by arsenic. A remedy that is strong enough to do good is almost invariably strong enough to do harm, if it be not used properly (*ibid.,* p. 288).

During 1860–1870 Darwin was treated first by Doctor William Brinton, whose chief specialty was in the field of gastro-enterology, and who has been described as one of the most cheery and skillful physicians of the day (F. Darwin, 1888: **3**: p. 1).

He was followed by Doctor Henry Bence Jones, a friend of Thomas Huxley and a probable friend of Benjamin Brodie (Huxley, 1900: **1**: p. 242; **2**: p. 390; Rosenbloom, 1919; Moreton, 1921), and, like Brinton, a highly respected physician. Bence Jones is best known today for the protein named after him. Around 1870 Sir Andrew Clark succeeded Bence Jones as Darwin's physician and he remained in that capacity until the death of his patient in 1882. While under the care of the latter two physicians Darwin suffered less distress and discomfort than he had during the preceding years, and he was able to work more steadily (F. Darwin, 1888: **3**: p. 355).

Doctor Andrew Clark has been praised for his scientific knowledge and his skill in providing relief and in curing the diseases of his patients. He was known for his experience in treating problems relating to the lungs, kidneys, and the digestive tract (Berdoe, 1893: p. 455). Sir Francis Darwin remembered him as a cheering influence upon his father and mentioned that the doctor's kindness and friendship were deeply appreciated by Darwin and his children (F. Darwin, 1888: **3**: p. 355). By the psychiatrist, Douglas Hubble, in his paper on Darwin and his suppressed hatred toward his father, Sir Andrew was seen in a rather different light. Referring at first to Dr. Bence Jones's recommendation that Darwin take up horseback riding, Hubble stated (1943: p. 130):

Darwin enjoyed these rides, but one day Tommy fell with him on Keston Common. "This upset his nerves and he was advised to give up riding." Unlucky Bence-Jones. From here, there was but one choice, inevitable and consoling: the Victorian sick found their ultimate haven in the comforting presence of Sir Andrew Clark.

One may wonder what prompted Hubble to expose himself in this manner. There is no positive information about the reason why Darwin left Bence Jones. To imply some petulance on Darwin's part because he fell from his horse is about as suspect an interpretation as is possible. Lawrence Kohn (1963: p. 244) believes the reason may be related to the state of Bence Jones's health, for the doctor died three years later. An investigation into the life of the doctor seems to confirm this view: "During the last years of his life he suffered great bodily weakness and at times had a little irritability of manner no doubt due to his physical ailment" (Rosenbloom, 1919: p. 264). As for Sir Andrew Clark being a comfort, this was quite true. After having suffered some thirty-five years from a crippling illness and probably being subjected to purgings, leechings, bloodlettings, and any number of other types of medication, it would not be surprising if Darwin found Sir Andrew's psychotherapeutic emphasis preferable. The picture of this doctor as the inevitable last resort of the Victorian sick may be partly true for that very reason. As for why Darwin chose this prominent physician above another, the answer is probably quite simple. He was a friend and doctor to many of the scientists and thinkers of the time. According to George Eliot he ministered ". . . to all the brain-workers . . ." (Gould, 1904: 2: p. 81). Huxley, who had been to school with Clark in 1846 (Huxley, 1900: 2: p. 390), thought very highly of his talents. By 1871 or 1872, at about the time when Darwin began to engage Clark, he became Huxley's physician, and he remained in that position for many years. It is therefore very likely that either Huxley or some other friend persuaded Darwin to try his services after Bence Jones became seriously ill.

Dr. Clark is best known for his emphasis on the importance of dieting and travel to cure "dyspeptic" ailments. The philosophy behind the views expressed in Sir James Clark's book, *The Sanative Influence of Climate,* was still in effect. Sir Joseph Hooker recalled the instructions given to him by Dr. Andrew Clark before he left on a trip to the Continent with his friend, Thomas Huxley. This was in 1873 at a time when Huxley was very ill. Clark's instructions specified what Huxley was to ". . . eat, drink, and avoid, how much he was to sleep and rest, how little to talk and walk, etc." (*ibid.* 1: p. 421), and at another time we learn that Clark had instructed Huxley ". . . always to drink tea and hot cake at 4:30 . . ." (*ibid.* **2**: p. 156). Another of the doctor's prescriptions was to take what Huxley called "Clark's pills" which contained strychnine, or quinine and strychnine, and he took them for a long time. They are mentioned as early as 1871 and as late as 1885 (*ibid.* **1**: p. 385; **2**: p. 100). Nor was the doctor against the use of other potentially toxic drugs. In 1881 he wrote in the *British Medical Journal* (1881: pp. 90–91): "In the first place, alcohol was a poison, as were also strychnia, arsenic, and opium, but, in certain small doses, these were useful in special circumstances. . . ." Since he was then prescribing strychnine for the very common complaint of dyspepsia, it would appear the "special circumstances" were not defined too narrowly, and the same might have been the case with arsenic which he mentioned and which was then one of the favorite remedies against many ailments. By this time, however, earlier doubts about the possible long-term effects of arsenic were being raised once again, and Clark's rather cautious statement may have reflected this.

SOME FAMOUS BRITISH DYSPEPTICS

IN THE VICTORIAN age an unusually large number of prominent people suffered from "dyspepsia," "hypochondria," and other forms of ill-defined chronic malaise. The major characteristics of certain forms of dyspepsia have already been described in an earlier quotation of Dr. James Clark. In his book, *Biographical Clinics*, George M. Gould discussed fourteen well-known figures who were chronically ill during a large portion of their lives and who shared a number of similar "dyspeptic" complaints. Ten out of the group were from England: Thomas De Quincey, Thomas Carlyle and his wife, Robert Browning, George Lewes, Margaret Fuller Ossoli, Herbert Spencer, Thomas Huxley, George Eliot (Marian Evans), and Charles Darwin. Many more could have been added. In general terms, part of their symptoms included (Gould 1904: **2**: p. 9): ". . . headache, insomnia, 'biliousness,' sick-headache, 'nervousness,' dejection, [and] indescribable suffering. . . ." Many of these individuals probably shared the same doctors.[10] The last three mentioned—Huxley, Eliot, and Darwin—were treated by Sir Andrew Clark,[11] and they all were said to have died as the result of heart ailments. Gould believed that the multitudinous symptoms which tormented each of the fourteen individuals were the result of eyestrain. Some of them probably did suffer from defective eyesight, but it has not been demonstrated that such a diverse array of complaints could have originated from this cause, and members of the medical profession who have in-

---

[10] In 1859 Huxley apparently knew Sir Henry Holland quite well (see F. Darwin, 1888: **2**: p. 251). It is possible Huxley was consulting with Holland at that time.
[11] Darwin and his brother, Erasmus, were ill during much of their adult lives. They both consulted Dr. Henry Holland. Thomas Carlyle and his wife, both chronic "dyspeptics," were close friends of Erasmus Darwin. Thomas Huxley became a friend of Herbert Spencer in 1852, and at about the same time Spencer established a friendship with George Eliot and G. H. Lewes. Huxley and Darwin were, of course, good friends. Thus many of the notable dyspeptics were joined together by direct and once-removed friendship with each other. Further investigation would probably reveal other relationships between this select group of ailing individuals.

vestigated Darwin's illness have rejected this hypothesis. Nevertheless, Gould performed a service by revealing the widespread nature of a malady which resembled in many ways Darwin's type of illness. The details of Thomas Huxley's ailment may be used to illustrate this point.

At the age of thirteen or fourteen Huxley sank into ". . . a strange state of apathy . . ." which he attributed to having been somehow poisoned while he was assisting in a post-mortem examination. Although he soon recovered from this state, he believed that the poison had permanently injured him, for he stated ". . . from that time my constant friend, hypochondriacal dyspepsia, commenced his half-century of co-tenancy of my fleshy tabernacle" (*ibid.*, 1903: 1: p. 109). At twenty-eight he found it necessary to regulate his daily routine in order to avoid having a headache which would last throughout the rest of the day (Huxley, 1900: 1: p. 113). A year later he wrote from a health resort that he was getting rid of his ". . . yellow face and putting on a brown one, banishing dyspepsias and hypochondrias" (*ibid.*, p. 123), and, in a letter to J. Tyndall written from the same resort about two months later (*ibid.*, p. 131):

> With you I envy Francis his gastric energies. I feel I have done for myself in that line, and am in for a life-long dyspeps. I have not, now, nervous energy enough for stomach and brain both, and if I work the latter, not even the fresh breezes of this place will keep the former in order. That is a discovery I have made here, and though highly instructive, it is not so pleasant as some other physiological results that have turned up.

One year later, Miss Heathorn, Huxley's bride-to-be, arrived in England from Australia. Her health was very poor and it was thought she might not live more than several months. Many years later, her son, Leonard Huxley, commented upon this (*ibid.*, p. 138):

> Miss Heathorn's health had broken down utterly and she looked at death's door. All through the preceding year she had been very ill; she had . . . caught a chill, and being wrongly treated by a doctor of the blood-letting, calomel-dosing school, she was reduced to a shadow, and only saved by another practitioner, who reversed the treatment just in time.

The idea that Huxley's wife, who was an invalid most of her life, may have been made ill by the medication common to that period, is an interesting one, and a point that will be returned to at a later time. It might be pointed out, however, that the ". . . blood-letting, calomel-dosing school . . ." was probably a shorthand description of the widespread practice of prescribing ". . . mercurials, arsenicals, antimonials and general blood-letting . . ." (see Wilder, 1901: p. 614, for example). The fact that Mrs. Huxley sometimes suffered from eczema (Huxley, 1900: **2**: p. 95) would suggest that she may have been given arsenic also (to be discussed later).

The years of 1857 and 1858 were particularly bad ones for the Huxleys. Their son, Leonard, described this period (*ibid.* **1**: p. 154):

Throughout this period his [i.e. Thomas's] health was greatly tried by the strain of his work and life in town. Headache! headache! is his repeated note in the early part of 1857, and in 1858 we find such entries as:—"Feb. 11.—Used up. Hypochondrical and bedevilled." "Ditto 12." "13—Not good for much." 21.—Toothache, incapable all day." And again:—March 30.—"Voiceless." "31.—Missed lecture." And, "April 1.—Unable to go out." He would come in thoroughly used up after lecturing twice on the same day, as frequently happened, and lie wearily on one sofa while his wife, whose health was wretched, matched him on the other. Yet he would go down to a lecture feeling utterly unable to deliver it, and, once started, would carry it through successfully—at what cost of nervous energy was known only to those two at home.

Even with all these complaints he believed that his health was better than it had been for some years, for he looked back on the preceding years as a time when he had had a great fear of becoming a ". . . confirmed dyspeptic . . ." (*ibid.,* p. 170). In 1862 he was once again writing of his unsatisfactory health and being teased by ". . . neuralgia or rheumatism or whatever it is" (*ibid.,* p. 253). He also went to bed for a period of ten days during this year because of an unaccountable prostration of strength which he attributed to an obstruction of the liver (Gould, 1903: **1**: p. 111). Like Darwin he sometimes looked well but felt terrible (Huxley, 1900: **1**: p. 273). By 1871, at the age of forty-six, he once again took a turn for the worse. One of the early signs of this change became apparent when his arms went black and blue under muscular strain (*ibid.*, p. 391). By the end of the year he suddenly broke down and could neither work nor think. He referred to himself as ". . . a poor devil whose brains and body are in a colloid state . . ." and in the same letter wrote: "God be with thee, . . . and strengthen the contents of thy gall-bladder!" (*ibid.*, p. 393). This condition remained with him, and by the next year he wrote that he had incessant dyspeptic nausea (*ibid.*, p. 396). Rest, travel, a special diet, and strict ascetic principles with regard to alcohol and tobacco provided only temporary relief: "I returned, thinking myself very well, but a bad fit of dyspepsia seized me, and I found myself obliged to be very idle and very careful of myself . . ." (*ibid.*, p. 402). During this time he kept early hours, and avoided both society and societies, and went for an hour's horseback ride in a park during the early morning, but all these experiments were useless. He explained it wasn't his brain but his stomach that was to blame (*ibid.*, pp. 401, 408). Phrases like being ". . . worried to death with dyspepsia and the hypochondriacal bedevilments that follow its train," and ". . . continuous dyspepsia and concurrent hypochondriacal incapacity" (*ibid.*, p. 411 etc.) are found in several of the letters to his friends. His advice to his wife at the time indicates that she was still in bad health: "I hope you are physically better. Look sharply after your diet, take exercise and defy the blue-devils, and you will weather the storm" (*ibid.*, p. 432).

In the autumn of 1873 he described his health as traveling between the two stations of dyspepsia and health and this condition apparently remained with him during the next several years. By 1884, at the age of fifty-nine, he was physically an old man (or, to borrow a phrase from Darwin who had described his own state many years before, he felt like a dull, old, spiritless dog). Leonard Huxley comments on this period (*ibid.* 2: p. 70):

From this time forward the burden of ill-health grew slowly and steadily. Dyspepsia and the hypochondriacal depression which follows its train, again attacked Huxley as they had attacked him twelve years before, though this time the physical misery was perhaps less. His energy was sapped; when his official work was over, he could hardly bring himself to renew the investigation in which he had always delighted. To stoop over the microscope was a physical discomfort. . . .

It was during this year he had all his remaining teeth removed (*ibid.,* p. 75). His own description of his state of health shows that he had not however lost his sense of humor. Referring to his intended visit to Penzance, he wrote: "I am possessed by seven devils—not only blue, but of the deepest indigo—and I shall try to transplant them into a herd of Cornish swine." And, in a letter written from Fowey in Cornwall a few days later: ". . . if I find myself picking up any good in these parts, I shall probably linger here or hereabouts. But a good deal will depend on the weather— inside as well as outside. I am convinced that the prophet Jeremiah (whose works I have been studying) must have been a flatulent dyspeptic—there is so much agreement between his views and mine" (*ibid.,* pp. 80–81, 85, 86).

It bothered Huxley that neither he nor Dr. Andrew Clark could find the slightest trace of an organic disease anywhere. The doctor diagnosed his problem as a slight affection of the liver and general nervous depression. Ten days later Huxley was to remark: "Clark's course of physic is lightening my abdominal troubles but I am preposterously weak with a kind of shabby brokendown indifference to everything . . .", and, contrary to the Doctor's opinion, he believed he would live two or three years at most. This prospect seemed preferable to having to endure a life of agonizing discomfort:

. . . it is better to wind up that way [i.e. dead] than to go growling out one's existence as a ventose hypochondriac, dependent upon the condition of a few square inches of mucous membrane for one's heaven or hell.

In a slightly lighter vein he referred to the question of death and the state of his liver:

The truth of the answer to Mallock's question "Is life worth living?" that depends on the liver—is being strongly enforced upon me in the hepatic sense of liver, and I must confess myself fit for very little (*ibid.,* pp. 85, 87, 94, 101, 102).

These conditions and his "weariness and deadness," nervous irritability, and decreasing ability to hear, encouraged him to shun company. Just as Darwin had been unable to attend his father's funeral many years before because of a fairly similar complaint, so Huxley wanted to beg out of having to attend his daughter's wedding (*ibid.,* p. 87): "I would give a great deal to be able to escape facing the wedding, for my nervous system is in the condition of that of a frog under opium." Since Dr. Clark prescribed this drug "under certain circumstances," Huxley may not have been speaking figuratively. He was also being given strychnine in the form of "Clark's pills" about this time.

Around June of 1885, at sixty years of age, Huxley had decided to resign his position as president of the Royal Society. He wrote that his condition was one of ". . . blue devils and funk—funk and blue devils. Liver, I expect," and later, in a letter to Sir M. Flower, he stated (*ibid.,* p. 114):

While undoubtedly much better in general health, I am in a curious state of discouragement, and I should like nothing better than to remain buried here (Bournemouth) or anywhere else, out of the way of trouble and responsibility.

Two years later he wrote of being bothered with muscular rheumatism and pleurisy. The pleurisy became so bad that he ". . . received imperative notice to quit town with all celerity." He first went to Ilkley, a health resort in Yorkshire which had been frequented by Darwin and many other distinguished chronically ill people, and then to Switzerland. There the muscular rheumatism reasserted itself and he also mentions having regular liver upsets (*ibid.,* pp. 176–177). The following year he detected a ". . . praecordial uneasiness and intermittent pulse . . .," and he was told by a Doctor Hames that he had a weakness and enlargement of his left ventricle. Consultation with another doctor the following year brought forth the comment: "H. Thompson . . . treats the notion that I ever had a dilated heart with scorn! Oh these doctors! they are worse than theologians" (*ibid.,* pp. 207, 253).

Between about 1890 and 1895 there are references to long periods of prostration, deafness, liver and lumbago troubles, neuralgia, severe lung trouble—bronchitis and influenza. The "influenza demon" was referred to as an old enemy of his, although there do not appear to have been many references to it in his published letters before that time. In March of 1895 he contracted a case of influenza with aches and pains, restless paroxysms of coughing, and general incapacity; it was followed by a severe case of bronchitis. The following four months were a painful struggle against disease. His heart was again affected and "renal mischief" ensued, and this was accompanied by distressing attacks of nausea and vomiting which sometimes lasted for hours. He died soon afterward (*ibid.,* pp. 307, 404–405, 415, 421, 423–425).

Another Victorian notable, George Eliot, shared Dr. Andrew Clark's services with Darwin, Huxley, and many other well-known figures, as has already been mentioned. Since she also frequented hydropathic establishments, such as Malvern (one of Darwin's favorites) and Ilkley (visited by Darwin and Huxley), it is quite possible that she and Darwin had had more than one physician in common. Her symptoms were even more diverse than those of Huxley. They included frequent headaches, sometimes of a violent variety, prolonged malaise (often used as a euphemism at this time for vomiting), indigestion, frequent colds and sore throats, heart palpitations, influenza, fatigue and feebleness, red and streaming eyes—possibly conjunctivitis—chills, "palsy," swimming head, insomnia, biliousness, lumbar neuralgia, backaches, "faceache," aching limbs, mental depression and melancholia, and acute laryngitis. Before she died in 1880 she mentioned having a renal disorder. Clark diagnosed her death as having been caused by pericarditis from sympathetic inflammation of acute laryngitis. Like Darwin and Huxley, she was thought to be a "dyspeptic." She found that "tonics" sometimes alleviated her problems (Gould, 1904: **2**: pp. 57–83).

All three—Darwin, Huxley, and George Eliot—spent the greater part of their lives struggling against the discomfort, fatigue, and mental depression of their respective illnesses. None of them were at all certain about the probable aetiology of their complaints, although Huxley at one time suspected he may have been poisoned in some mysterious way, and Darwin believed his illness may have been related to an inherited weakness. They had many symptoms in common with each other and with the other Victorian dyspeptics already mentioned. Darwin's symptoms, which have not been discussed in detail up to now, appear to be almost a prototype of this type of illness. These will now be examined.

DARWIN'S SYMPTOMS

W HEN DARWIN was in London making last minute preparations for his forthcoming voyage on the *Beagle* he wrote
to his sister Susan requesting that she send to him certain items,
including a little book on taxidermy. He then went on to state
(F. Darwin, 1888: **1**: p. 206):

> Ask my father if he thinks there would be any objection to my taking
> arsenic for a little time, as my hands are not quite well, and I have *always
> observed* that if I once get them well, and change my manner of living
> about the same time, they will generally remain well. What is the dose?
> [Italics added.]

Implied in this statement is the fact that he had taken arsenic
before and found it an effective cure against whatever was wrong
with his hands. Professor A. W. Woodruff (1965: p. 745) has
interpreted Darwin's reference to mean that he had a tremor of his
hands with possibly some degree of dermatitis, and Lady Nora
Barlow (1945: p. 45) has suggested that he was referring to his
trouble with eczema.

In 1882 Darwin's old schoolfriend, John M. Herbert, recalled
that Charles had taken arsenic while he was a student at Cambridge, and this was not to cure his hands (Darwin Papers, no. 112,
1882):

> He had at one time an eruption about his mouth for which he took
> small doses of arsenic. He told me that he had ment d. this treatment to
> his Father & that his Father had warned him that the cure might be
> attended with worse consequences—I forget what he said the risk was but
> I think it was partial paralysis.

Mention of having had trouble with his lips during these years
is also found in several of Darwin's published letters. Francis
Darwin, in referring to one of these letters, stated that his father
was probably suffering from eczema of the lips (F. Darwin, 1888:
1: p. 178). Arsenic is still considered to be useful in treating
chronic and atopic eczema. Wiener (1955: pp. 188, 252) points

43

out that some surprising results can be obtained from its use, although the results can never be predicted. He also makes the interesting observation that because it is very effective in some cases of psoriasis (and this would apply to eczema), the patient will often insist on its use again in recurrences of his affliction; if this is permitted, sooner or later manifestations of chronic arsenic poisoning will develop.

It is of interest to relate the statement by Herbert on Darwin's use of arsenic in Cambridge, to Darwin's later request that his father approve his use of this drug for his hands. Robert Darwin probably did not prescribe arsenic for the condition of his son's lips, and he disapproved of its continued use. His son's later request indicates that Charles also had used it to cure his hand ailment and that it had been temporarily effective. The request was clearly an appeal to his father to change his mind on the subject. This appeal probably failed, for in the next letter to his sister Susan, Darwin wrote that he did not think he would take any arsenic (F. Darwin, 1888: **1**: p. 210). His continued desire to take the drug, even though his father had warned him of the possible long-term consequences, reveals the extent to which he believed in the efficacy of arsenic as a means of curing his lip and hand ailments.

Doctor Henry Holland was apparently visited by Charles from Cambridge at the end of February in 1829 (*ibid.*, p. 175) and, in a letter written one month later (*ibid.*, p. 176), we learn that Charles had been suffering from a bout of lip trouble which had contributed to his depressed spirits at the time. Since Darwin consulted Holland soon after his return from the voyage around the world, it is more than likely his February visit was to obtain professional advice relating to his lip trouble and that Holland had prescribed the arsenic.[12] A few months after his first mention of

---

[12] An alternative explanation may be that Darwin prescribed it for himself. It will be remembered that before he left for Edinburgh he had helped treat his father's patients and, with the advice of his father, had "made up" the medicines himself. During the voyage around the world, he also made numerous notations to purchase medicines (to be discussed), and at a later time recommended to a friend of his

lip trouble he was severely troubled again with the same affliction while on an entomological trip to North Wales. As during his first-mentioned attack, he found it necessary to hibernate (*ibid.*, p. 179):

The first two days I went on pretty well, taking several good insects; but for the rest of that week my lips became suddenly so bad, and I myself not very well, that I was unable to leave the room, and on the Monday I retreated with grief and sorrow back again to Shrewsbury.

With this type of attack there would have been plenty of incentive to have quietly disregarded his father's admonition. Although this attack was undoubtedly much milder than those he experienced in later years, there is probably a genetic relationship between the two. His later attacks, which were referred to as vasomotor nerve storms, or periodic crises (*The British Medical Journal*, 1882: p. 628), were described by his friend Sir Joseph Hooker (1899: p. 188):

As his health fluctuated or declined, and especially during his sharper attacks of illness, these interviews [with Hooker] became intermittent. . . . These morning interviews were followed by his taking a complete rest, for they always exhausted him, and sometimes what he called "stars in the eyes," the latter too often the prelude of violent eczema in the head, during which time he was hardly recognisable.

Some of the reasons why arsenic was prescribed during the period of Darwin's early and middle adult years were touched upon in the discussion of the physicians of that time. A complete list of indications is very extensive: intermittent and periodical headaches, tic douloureux, various types of neuralgia arising from malaria, ague, brow ague, disorders of the uterus, and many different skin disorders. Applied externally, it was used to destroy warts and tumors. Arsenic was also mentioned as being an excellent tonic and was supposed to give firmness and vigor to the constitu-

that he externally apply the *"deadly Poison,"* Tincture of Arnica, and other drugs, in order to alleviate the pain of a toothache (in Stecher, 1961: p. 203). A letter written to Asa Gray in 1864 reveals that he was on the lookout for new medicines —in this case he was enquiring about "Syrup of Phosphates," a new Philadelphia medicine he had heard about (in Loewenberg, 1939: p. 56).

tion. At various times during the nineteenth century, and later, it was also used for the following ailments: anemia, pernicious anemia, epilepsy, tuberculosis, diabetes, leukemia, asthma, malaria, chronic heart affections, nutritional disturbances, migraine, goiter, neurasthenia, hysteria, cancer, rheumatism, arthritis, multiple sclerosis, syphilis, "sluggish body combustion," and many skin disorders. In this latter category were such afflictions as acute and chronic eczema, psoriasis, pemphigus, acne, dermatitis herpetiformis, and lichen planus.

In 1786 Thomas Fowler wrote an article on the use of arsenic in medicine, entitled, "Medical reports on the effects of arsenic in the cure of agues, remitting fevers, and periodic headaches." His arsenic-based formula became known as Fowler's solution; it consisted of potassium arsenite (arsenic trioxide) flavored slightly with oil of lavender and tincture of cinnamon (Boos, 1939: p. 36). It became very popular for the reasons mentioned in the title of his report and also as a tonic for skin, nerves, blood, and general health. In the Fens it became a favorite prophylactic against ague, being used daily by many people (Duncan, 1804: p. 176; Hutchinson, 1887: p. 1280). The tradition of its use was therefore well established in Cambridge.

Other early advocates of arsenic as a medicine were Thomas Girdlestone, Christian Friedrich Harles, and Laurent-Theódore Biett, all of whom were influential during the early part of the nineteenth century in popularizing its internal use for skin diseases. Biett recommended the use of iron and arsenic together for this purpose (Mettler and Mettler, 1947: pp. 654, 674). Other medical preparations which contained arsenic included Donovan's solution (arsenic and mercuric iodides), de Valagin's solution (liquor arsenii chloridi), and sodium cacodylate (Vallee, Ulmer and Wacker, 1960: p. 133).

One of the unfortunate aspects of the medicinal use of arsenic is that it may deceptively provide temporary relief for what it may later aggravate, or, in fact, create in another individual. It was taken to improve general health, to diminish exhaustion, improve the appetite, alleviate nervous disorders, and improve body combustion. It is well documented that over a period of time it frequently does just the opposite: it produces a state of cachexia, encourages great fatigue, significantly diminishes the appetite, creates many different nervous disorders, and is commonly associated with gastro-intestinal disturbances. The same may be stated for its use to alleviate headaches, arthritis, anemia, epileptiform seizures, heart problems, and certain skin disorders. As an example, it has been reported that new lesions resembling psoriatic patches may arise in psoriasis for which the arsenic was given (Beerman, 1946: p. 497), and that psoriasis may appear when individuals have been exposed to arsenic trichloride and trioxide (von Oettingen, 1958: p. 34). When used for eczema it may provide temporary relief but may also create a common chronic condition known as "eczema arsenicalis" (Blyth and Blyth, 1920: p. 577; see also Buchanan, 1962: pp. 19–20). Darwin's use of this medicine to attempt to cure what has been interpreted as eczema of the lips and hands is particularly interesting in this regard. The clinical picture may have been quite complicated.

Although orthodox opinion has largely favored a psychogenic origin of Darwin's illness, there have been a number of attempts to identify an organic cause. Several writers have suggested that his debilitating seasickness during the voyage of the *Beagle* affected him for the rest of his life (see F. Darwin, 1888: **1**: p. 224; Romanes, 1882: p. 51; Johnston, 1901: p. 157). Other individuals have stated that he may have had Chagas's disease (Adler, 1959 and 1965), brucellosis which became chronic (G. G. Simpson, 1958: p. 121), malaria (Greenacre, 1963: p. 32, see also Barlow, 1945: p. 211), appendicitis, a duodenal ulcer, pyorrhea (Barlow, 1958: p. 241), a peptic ulcer, inherited neurasthenia (Alvarez, 1943 and 1959), and gout (see Stetten, 1959: p. 195, for example). In some of these cases the organic cause was seen as underlying an important neurotic element.

One of the major difficulties with all of these views is that some of the important symptoms of Darwin's post-voyage illness were already in evidence before he set foot aboard the *Beagle.* During the months of October and November of 1831 he was preparing for his departure from England. Most of October was spent in London and all of November in Plymouth and the surrounding area. In his pocket notebook he noted: "These months very miserable" (F. Darwin, 1888: **1:** p. 191). On November 15 he wrote (Barlow, 1967: p. 48): ". . . I have only now to pray for the sickness to moderate its fierceness, and I shall do very well." It is not possible to know the nature of this prolonged illness but the use of the term "fierceness" to describe it would suggest he may have been referring to an attack of eczema and its syndrome, such as he had apparently experienced in Cambridge earlier. Hooker, it will be recalled, referred to Darwin's later attacks of eczema as being "violent," and Darwin had once referred to the condition of his lips as becoming "suddenly so bad." As late as September 6 he had referred to the bad state of his hands, which may have meant that he was suffering from eczema at that time. The fact that he had had some miserable affliction while he was in London would tend to rule out the idea that he was referring to cardiac pain and palpitations. In his autobiography he appears to fix the beginning of this trouble after he had left London and had taken up residence in Plymouth (Barlow, 1958: p. 79).

The psychologist Dr. Rankine Good mentioned that Darwin had had "an occasional attack of palpitation" when he was a student at Cambridge (Good, 1954*a:* p. 107). He did not give his source and the present writer has not been able to discover one. The first well-known record of heart trouble is that just mentioned in connection with Darwin's temporary residence in Plymouth in 1831. He refers to this in his autobiography (Barlow, 1958: pp. 79–80):

I was . . . troubled with palpitation and pain about the heart, and like many a young ignorant man, especially one with a smattering of medical knowledge, was convinced I had heart disease. I did not consult any doctor, as I fully expected to hear the verdict that I was not fit for the voyage; and I was resolved to go at all hazards.

His comment to J. D. Hooker in 1837 that anything which flurried him completely knocked him up and brought on a violent palpitation was quoted earlier. In 1863, at the age of fifty-four, he mentioned being ". . . not a little uncomfortable from frequent uneasy feeling of fullness, slight pain and tickling about the heart. But as I have no other symptoms of heart complaint I do not suppose it is affected . . ." (F. Darwin, 1888: **3**: p. 15). His diagnosis was probably essentially correct.

During the five years following his first recognized cardiac complaint in Plymouth he underwent extreme exertion at many different times, for example on his ascent of Mount Tarn and another high mountain in the area around Tierra del Fuego. The present writer has climbed 2,600-foot high Mount Tarn in the company of an experienced rock-climber and a cross-country runner, and all of us were thoroughly exhausted. Almost impenetrable dense stands of trees strewn with prone, partially decayed logs, and intersected by very steep and slippery-sided ravines made the going very difficult in the lower elevations near the Strait of Magellan. Succeeding this were thickets of brush and then open country consisting of bogs and yielding ground cover. With each step the downward movement into the spongy mass was about equivalent to the distance progressed. Scree and talus are found in the highest elevations and the angle of ascent is steep and exhausting. In 1827 Captain Philip Parker King made this same climb and mentions finding the ". . . fatigue very oppressive . . ." and some of the men accompanying him ". . . suffered much, from being unused to such exercise" (King, 1839: p. 40).

Darwin's ascent up the beautiful Tuauru (Tiaauru) Valley in Tahiti near Point Venus was probably even more demanding. An experienced and fit climber in that area, Monsieur M. F. A. Jay of Arue, Tahiti, informed the present writer that it would not be possible to follow Darwin's route up the valley today because the trails have not been kept open, but even if they had been cleared to the point where the steep ascent begins, he found it difficult to believe that such a journey could have been made by Darwin.[13] Almost certainly the two and one-half day trek up and down very steep and slippery slopes could only have been accomplished by someone with a fundamentally sound heart. George Forster's narrative of his walk up part of the same valley makes an interesting comparison with Darwin's acount. He and his companion ended up giving their fowling-pieces to their native guide and were forced to lean upon him in difficult places; other natives were summoned from the valley bottom to bring up refreshments to the weary naturalists (Forster, 1777: **1**: pp. 350–351). Mount Wellington in Tasmania, over 4,100 feet in altitude (Darwin erroneously stated it was 3,100 feet), and Green Hill on Ascencion Island, over 2,800 feet high (which he apparently climbed with "a bounding step"—Barlow, 1958: p. 82), were Darwin's last two strenuous climbs undertaken before arriving in England. The first of these was ascended along the more difficult damp side.

One year after Darwin's return to England, and six years after his last-known similar complaint, we read in the already-quoted letter to J. D. Hooker that he was being bothered by heart palpitations. Not long after that—under ten months—he went on a geomorphological excursion to the valleys of Glen Roy and Glen Gloy in Scotland. He ". . . wandered all over the mountains in all directions . . ." and, as A. W. Woodruff has pointed out, reached a height of at least 2,200 feet. The mountains are steep in this district and the going is arduous. In the summer of 1842 he went to Northern Wales to study the glacial geomorphology of the region and climbed a number of mountains, including one ". . . very steep mountain . . ." east-northeast of the upper lake within the Vale of Llanberis (Darwin, 1842: p. 361)—probably

---

[13] When Darwin took the trip the natives knew of a hidden route up the steeper part by way of a series of ledges. They also used ropes over the most difficult section. This information may not have been passed on to the present inhabitants.

the peak north of Y Garn whose elevation is over 2,700 feet. Professor Woodruff also noted the significance of the fact that in later years, while in residence at Down House, Darwin kept the key to his snuffbox in the cellar and the snuffbox in the attic, for the purpose of reducing his consumption of snuff.[14] The walk from the cellar to the attic is long and the stairs leading to the attic are sufficiently steep to be a real chore. This, together with the occasional alacrity of his movements in later years, argues against his having had heart disease at least until his later middle years, and probably not for several years after that. In March of 1863 he was troubled again by palpitations and pain about his heart but his doctor, William Brinton, declared in November of that year that neither his brain nor heart was primarily affected by his chronic illness. A few years later, Dr. Bence Jones found nothing wrong with his heart and recommended that he take up horseback riding, as previously mentioned (Woodruff, 1968: pp. 669–670; F. Darwin, 1888: **3**: pp. 1–2, 15).

Doctor Saul Adler's theory that Darwin may have had Chagas's disease from having been bitten while in Argentina by the blood-sucking insect, *Triatoma infestans* (the Benchuca bug), is also jeopardized by these facts (see Woodruff, 1968: pp. 67–72). According to Sir Peter Medawar the trypanosome invades the muscle of the heart in over eighty per cent of patients with this disease. Although Sir Peter favors Adler's theory, he also combines it with a significant neurotic component for Darwin's illness; he remarks that it is a little surprising that the acute fever and glandular swellings which typically follow such an infection were never mentioned. That such a prolonged infection without either host or parasite gaining the upper hand is also mentioned as being unusual (Medawar, 1967: pp. 65–66; see also, Woodruff, 1965; p. 747; Woodruff, 1968: pp. 670–672).

---

[14] H. J. Roberts lists the use of snuff as a stimulant as one of the possible signs of a narcoleptic individual (1967: p. 162). Darwin began taking snuff quite early in life. It is reported that he used it when he was a student at Edinburgh, and both "snuff" and "snuff box" are to be found in a shopping list written in 1833 (F. Darwin, 1888: **1**: p. 122; Barlow, 1945: p. 206).

There is also some evidence to suggest that Darwin was occasionally unusually susceptible to fatigue even as a young man. A trip to Birmingham in October of 1829 to attend a music meeting, and, incidentally, to visit with some of his relatives, was referred to by him as having ". . . knocked me up most dreadfully . . ." (F. Darwin, 1888: 1: p. 180), and this was at about the time when he probably began to take arsenic for his eczema. There are also other references to being ". . . so tired . . ." and ". . . very much fatigued & am going to bed" (September 2 and 3, 1831) ; it was on September 6, 1831, that he wrote to his sister requesting that she ask his father what dosage of arsenic to use to cure his hands. However, since he had just learned of his father's approval of his move to become the *Beagle's* naturalist, and he had also just traveled some distance, it is also possible the fatigue experienced was not unusual (*ibid.,* pp. 199, 201, 206; Barlow, 1933: p. 3; see also Woodruff, 1965; p. 745).

It may therefore be stated with some certainty that before Darwin left England he had already manifested some of the symptoms which in later life became chronic. These included periodic attacks of eczema during which he felt unwell and depressed and secluded himself; an unspecified illness which lasted for two months prior to his departure from England and which was so bad that he wished it would ". . . moderate its fierceness . . ."; an attack of cardiac palpitation and pain; and, possibly, an unusual susceptibility to fatigue at certain times. Within a very short time after his arrival in South America he also became infected with a bad case of boils (to be discussed), a condition which periodically plagued him after his return to England.

There are some curious unanswered questions about the nature of Darwin's seasickness which may be related to the former discussion. Five days before taking the steamer to Plymouth with Captain FitzRoy to see the *Beagle* for the first time (F. Darwin, 1888: 1: p. 190), and over a month and one-half before his first visit to the ship as its naturalist, he wrote to his sister, Susan (*ibid.,* p. 207): "I daresay you expect I shall turn back at the Madeira: if I have a morsel of stomach left, I won't give up." The anticipation that he would unduly suffer from seasickness is an interesting one. It may be that an earlier experience in crossing the English Channel had indicated that he was unusually sensitive to the motion of the sea; on the other hand, it is also possible that he recognized he was predisposed to nausea and vomiting. There is a possibility that these same symptoms might have been part of the syndrome related to his eczema attacks. In a letter to Asa Gray in 1864 he wrote that he no longer vomited daily and that his head hardly troubled him any more except for ringing in the ears (Loewenberg, 1939: p. 53). At the time he was in the midst of a three-months siege of illness (F. Darwin, 1888: **3:** p. 27). The reference to the state of his head may have meant that he had been afflicted by the type of eczema that made him barely recognizable. If so, eczema and vomiting sometimes probably went hand in hand, and his letter to his sister anticipating undue sensitivity to the motion of the sea makes more sense. It was in this same letter that he made mention of the state of his hands and it was soon thereafter that he suffered from two months of bad health. The idea that he may have been unusually susceptible to nausea prior to the voyage has already been advocated by George M. Gould and A. W. Woodruff (Gould, 1903: **1:** pp. 90–94; Woodruff, 1965: p. 747). Professor Woodruff believed Darwin's letter of the fifteenth of November, 1831, in which he stated that he hoped his sickness would moderate its fierceness, referred to this condition.

The prognostication of severe nausea and vomiting during the course of the voyage was fulfilled. This is attested to by Darwin's own notes and the recollections of some of his shipmates, such as Admiral J. Lort Stokes and Mr. A. B. Usborne (F. Darwin, 1888: **1:** p. 224). The latter wrote that he remembered Darwin as ". . . a dreadful sufferer from sea-sickness . . ." and Stokes remembered with sympathy the agony of his friend and attributed his later state of chronic ill health to the effect of the voyage. According to a letter written by Darwin not too long before the close of the voyage his suffering had become worse than it had been during the earlier part of the voyage. This is out of phase with the view he expressed to his son, Francis, in later years. He then told his son that he was uncomfortable when the *Beagle* pitched heavily but was only ill for the first three weeks of the voyage. He also rejected the idea that his health had been affected by such a cause, as was commonly believed by some of his friends [15] (*ibid.*, p. 223). The answer to this enigma may well relate to the question of his possible early predisposition to nausea. In one sense it may be claimed that he had symptoms resembling *mal de mer* during much of his life following his return home from the voyage, for he had frequent attacks of nausea and vomiting, sometimes daily, and he was apprehensive that his stomach would fail while he was in public (Browne, 1943: p. 14; F. Darwin, 1888: **1**: p. 345, 383–384; Loewenberg, 1939: p. 53). The suggestion that he may have had a similar complaint before the voyage began is also a consideration; further, he occasionally suffered from bouts of vomiting while traveling on land in South America (to be discussed). Darwin would have recognized the similarity of these symptoms on land and at sea. In so far as this condition would have been aggravated at sea, he may have preferred to describe it as seasickness. Alternatively, he may not have fully recognized the similarity of his symptoms until he had been back in England for a period of time. In either case, the discrepancy between what was recorded and later remembered about the voyage would be obviated.

Darwin suffered from several attacks of illness during the time he spent in South America. The first of these occurred in Bahia within a few days after his first landfall on the continent. He had pricked his knee and his leg became swollen, much inflamed, and very painful, and he was confined to his hammock for eight days

---

[15] This is another reason for suspecting that Darwin was not a hypochondriac. If he had been one it would seem likely that he would have welcomed their suggestion.

(Barlow, 1933: p. 42; 1945: p. 60). Judging from a subsequent description of a similar attack, he probably had a large boil or carbuncle. One month later, on a trip to the tropical forest near Macae (northeast of Cabo Frio) in Brazil, he wrote that he had felt ". . . feverish, shivering and sickness [16]—much exhausted: could eat nothing . . . miserably faint and troubled with faintness. . . . Felt very ill. . . ." He stated that he recovered during the following day with the help of cinnamon and port wine, and, perhaps, some of the medicines in his host's well supplied cabinet (Barlow, 1945: pp. 160–161). A month later he was ". . . almost laid up by an inflammation in my arm. Any small prick is very apt to become in this country a painful boil." This lasted for four days (Barlow, 1933: p. 61). About three months later he mentioned experiencing a bad headache (*ibid.,* p. 87). In October of 1833 he suffered from a sharp attack of fever in Santa Fé (northwest of Buenos Aires): "Unwell in the night, today feverish and very weak from great heat . . . very much exhausted . . . very unwell in bed . . . unwell in bed . . . find myself much tired." He wrote to his sister Caroline, that most of the fifteen days of this expedition were ones of uncommon fatigue. Because of his illness he decided to travel by river boat to Buenos Aires rather than to travel overland (Barlow, 1945: pp. 64, 208–209).

With the exception of spending a day indoors because of a disordered stomach (*ibid.,* p. 213) and two days of being very feverish following a period of extreme exertion (Barlow, 1933: p. 205), there appears to be no mention of illness (apart from "seasickness") for another year. In the latter part of September in 1834, while on a trip in the general vicinity of Santiago, Chile, he wrote that he began to feel very unwell. His stomach was in a bad state and he felt exceedingly exhausted (*ibid.,* p. 240; Barlow, 1945: pp. 107, 228). With the help of a carriage he arrived in Valparaiso and was there placed in bed and treated by

---

[16] A term he used for vomiting (see his letter to his sister, Susan, for example, in Barlow, 1945: p. 49).

the acting surgeon of the *Beagle,* Mr. Bynoe. About three weeks after the onset of the illness Darwin wrote to his sister, Caroline: ". . . Bynoe, with a good deal of Calomel and rest, has nearly put me right again, & I am now only a little feeble." His improved condition lasted only a short while. About one month later he wrote that he had been forced to go back to bed for another two weeks, and as late as March 10, 1835, some four months after he had resumed his normal activities, he noted that his stomach, ". . . partly from sea-sickness & partly from my illness in Valparaiso is not very strong" (Barlow, 1945: pp. 106–107, 109, 115). Shortly after this he noted that he had not felt very well for an eight-day period (April 9 to 17, 1835) and had seen nothing and admired nothing during that time (Barlow, 1933: p. 306). In later years his son, Francis, reported that his father had informed him that ". . . every secretion of the body was affected . . ." during the prolonged illness in Valparaiso (F. Darwin, 1888: **1**: p. 224); the liberal use of calomel would have contributed to this state.

It has already been noted that the administration of calomel for a number of different complaints was a common medical practice during that time. Even though the ship's surgeon had administered this medicine to Darwin, it may have been partly at his patient's suggestion. A shopping list written by Darwin during the previous year included the reminder: "Buy knife, Prometheans, medicine, Calomel" (Barlow, 1945: p. 184). He may also have favored emetics as a general type of medication, for only a few years before he had been given the responsibility of treating a number of his father's patients and had apparently prescribed tartar emetic for an entire family. He believed the results to have been successful and felt quite proud over his accomplishment (Barlow, 1958: p. 47).

In addition to the cures already mentioned—calomel, and cinnamon and port wine—he found ". . . much mattee and smoking . . ." to be very useful in alleviating muscle cramps (Barlow,

1945: p. 201). His shopping lists often reminded him to buy medicines and pills of unspecified types. One of the most interesting of these was more specific. It included such items as a preparation of opium and a truss (*ibid.*, p. 252):

> . . . .
> Drug . . .
> Dentist [mentioned in a number
>   of previous lists]
> Peppermint—Hops
> Carb. of soda—Laudanum—Lozenges
> ½ oz. Tic Jem. Muriaticae
> Lavender water [17] & Truss

[17] Fowler's solution is composed of arsenic, cinnamon, and oil of lavender. Darwin had used cinnamon and port wine as a cure against fever in Brazil. From the comments made before he left England, and from the fact that he undoubtedly had arsenic available from his taxidermy supplies, it is likely he possessed all of the ingredients to concoct his own Fowler's solution.

DARWIN AND ARSENIC

THE DISCUSSION has so far dealt with the following subjects (though not in the same order): (*a*) the nature of the medical profession and medication during the years of Darwin's illness; (*b*) the known medication and type of treatment preferred by some of Darwin's physicians and other prominent physicians of that time; (*c*) the rather common occurrence of similar symptoms, sometimes referred to as dyspepsia or hypochondria, at that period; (*d*) the early symptoms of illness manifested by Darwin and a certain similarity of these with those which developed after his return to England from the voyage around the world; (*e*) the use of arsenic by Darwin during presumed attacks of eczema and his belief that it was beneficial even though his father had warned him against its use; (*f*) evidence of Darwin's habit of purchasing and probably prescribing medicines for himself during the voyage; and, (*g*) a summary of most of the hypotheses involving a psychological aetiology of Darwin's illness and the reasons why it is believed they are inadequate. It has been broadly hinted throughout much of the discussion that the use of arsenic and other highly toxic forms of medication during those times may have been a major factor in producing a peculiarly Victorian type of "dyspepsia" and may also have significantly contributed to Darwin's physical ills. In an interesting review of the subject of Darwin's ill-health in the *Bulletin of the History of Medicine,* Lawrence Kohn examined a number of plausible theories on the subject, and incidentally made the following suggestion (1963: p. 252):

A far-fetched suggestion is that if he had continued to take arsenic which was prescribed for him as a young man, he might have developed chronic intoxication. The intestinal symptoms might be stretched to fit, but other significant findings such as skin pigmentation and generalized hair loss might have to be adduced to interest a modern coroner.

That Darwin took arsenic while he was a student at Cambridge was apparently unknown to Kohn, whose statement seems to have been based upon the letter in which Darwin asked his father's permission to use arsenic to attempt to cure his hand trouble. In view of the fact that arsenic was one of the more popular types of skin and tonic medicines of that period, and was widely used for many of the diverse complaints Darwin manifested, the idea is actually not far-fetched at all. The question is, how closely did Darwin's symptoms fit the pattern of chronic arsenic poisoning? The answer, which forms the basis of the discussion to follow, is that every one of his many and varied symptoms has been noted in individuals with this form of poisoning, and a large proportion of them are typical.

In the following list, items indicated by "A" are Darwin's symptoms, and those indicated by "B" are comparable symptoms which may occur in chronic arsenic poisoning.

1.

A. *Eczema;* attacks sometimes violent; probably dating as far back as his student days at Cambridge and intermittently occurring until he was an old man. (*British Med. Jour.,* 1882: p. 628; Hooker, 1899: p. 188).

B. Eczematoid complaints are very common. The exanthem has been called "eczema arsenicale" (Buchanan, 1962: p. 19; Blyth and Blyth, 1920: p. 577; C. K. Simpson, 1964: p. 276; Beerman, 1949: pp. 448–449; Leschke, 1934: p. 65).

2.

A. *Boils;* painful succession of attacks; bedridden with them; one described as "very large"; they were permitted to burst spontaneously and no antiseptic was used (Browne, 1943: p. 14; de Beer, 1959: **2**, 18: p. 12; Foster, 1965: p. 477; F. Darwin and Seward, 1903: **1**: p. 109; F. Darwin, 1888: **2**: pp. 221–222). In 1847? Darwin wrote: ". . . at present I am suffering from four boils and swellings, one of which hardly allows me the use of my right arm, and has stopped all my work, and dampened my spirits" (F. Darwin, 1888: **1:** p. 352). Many years later he wrote: "I have had a series of calamities; first a sprained ankle, and then a badly swollen whole leg and face, much rash, and a frightful succession of boils—four or five at once. I have felt quite ill, and have little faith in this 'unique crisis,' as the doctor calls it, doing me much good . . ." (*ibid.* **2:** pp. 221–222). He also suffered from boils when he was in Brazil.

B. Boils are commonly related to eczematoid disorders; they also occur in individuals who are chronically weak, exhausted, have lost much weight owing to illness, or suffer from nervous strain, all of which apply to chronic arsenic poisoning, e.g., Darwin. At least thirty varieties of skin eruption have been produced by various kinds of arsenicals; frequently-mentioned types are pustular, acneiform, vesicular eruptions, erythema multiforme, and various bullous conditions. These eruptions may be generalized or limited to certain areas of the neck and face (Farquharson, 1880: p. 802; Locket, 1957; p. 545; von Oettingen, 1958: p. 29; Ormsby and Montgomery, 1954: pp. 376–377; Cushny, 1947: p. 168).

3.

A. *Swellings;* swollen leg and face; non-use of arm caused by boils and swellings (see quotations in no. 2-A above).

B. Soft, pitting edema is fairly common among individuals with chronic arsenic intoxication. Out of 41 patients suffering from this form of poisoning and studied by Heyman, Pfeiffer, Willett and Taylor (1956: p. 403), 14 presented this condition. It was reported to have appeared within a week of the onset of arsenical neuritis and was usually confined to the feet and legs, occasionally becoming more generalized and involving the face, trunk, and arms. Vallee, Ulmer and Wacker (1960: p. 141) refer to the same condition as occurring in the legs, feet, or periorbital regions. Edema of the eyelids is very common. A reddening of the skin, or erythema, which is commonly related to this form of poisoning is sometimes associated with edema and swelling (von Oettingen, 1958: p. 30; C. K. Simpson, 1964: p. 276). A description of swellings associated with a patient taking an arsenical "cure" which is very much like the description of Darwin's condition in 2-A was quoted by Dr. Henry Hunt: ". . . my body and limbs were much swollen, and covered with erysipelas [streptococcal infection of the skin]: my hands and feet underwent a complete desquamation . . . an abscess formed under the affected arm, and several large pustules . . . broke out on the temples" (Hunt, 1844: p. 179). With the degeneration of the heart resulting from the ingestion of arsenic over a period of time, circulatory insufficiency with edema may result (Leschke, 1934: p. 68).

4.

A. *Rash;* sometimes described as severe; apparently quite common (see last quotation in 2-A above; Foster, 1965: p. 477). This might have been his term for eczema, or it may have referred to an erythematous condition or to desquamation over part of his body.

B. Simple erythema and exfoliative dermatitis are fairly common symptoms of chronic arsenical intoxication (von Oettingen, 1958; pp. 29, 33; Locket, 1957: p. 545; Moeschlin, 1965: p. 167; McNally, 1937: p. 237). The occurrence of eczematoid manifestations has already been discussed in 1-B.

5.

A. Probable *multiple corn-like elevations* on his hands. These are not mentioned in the literature, but an examination of the enlarged portion of the photograph of Darwin at the age of fifty-one in the frontispiece of Lady Barlow's edition of his autobiography (Barlow, 1958), appears to reveal several distinct eminences on his hands. His right hand reveals these above his thumb and index finger, and his left hand may exhibit one or more on the outside fleshy region above his fifth finger, although the latter is by no means certain. Later photographs of his face show a wart-like feature on his right cheek.

B. Multiple horny keratoses are very common among individuals who have taken small doses of arsenic. They characteristically form on the thenar eminences and lateral borders and backs of the fingers and over the phalangeal joints, and also on the heels and toes. When thus situated they may be regarded ". . . as almost pathognomic of chronic arsenical poisoning" (Buchanan, 1962: p. 106). According to at least one source, arsenical keratoses may develop as early as one month after taking arsenic or not until thirty years after the medication has been stopped. In addition to keratoses on the extremities, they are sometimes found on the trunk, face, and scalp. Once they develop they usually persist and about 20 per cent or more of the cases become cancerous (Ormsby and Montgomery, 1954: pp. 850–851). Another study indicated that out of 262 patients treated with arsenic between six and twenty-six years before, characteristic keratoses of the palms and soles were found in over 40 per cent, and these often revealed histological evidence of intra-epidermal carcinoma (*British Med. Jour.,* 1968: p. 191). Vallee, Ulmer and Wacker (1960: p. 145) believe there is little relation between the amount and duration of arsenical medication and the likelihood of the development of cancer. They also place the mean age of the appearance of keratosis at thirty-two years (after the first use of arsenic?).

6.

A. *Brown complexion.* Darwin's daughter, Henrietta Litchfield, wrote: "All through my father's middle age, his . . . brown out-of-doors complexion, so deceived his friends [about the real state of his health] . . ." (Litchfield, 1915: **2:** p. 60). She also mentioned that his eyes were clear gray-blue; this, and the fact that he stayed indoors much of the time, make it difficult to understand the color of his complexion. It is also interesting to note that she appears to limit this color to his middle age. Other observers, such as Henry Fairfield Osborn, stated that Darwin had a ". . . very ruddy face . . ." when he was an old man (Osborn, 1909: p. 340). "Ruddy" is sometimes used as a synonym for "tanned." If, in fact, the term was being used in its more commonly accepted sense, it might indicate a copper-colored hue or that the brown color of his middle years had been replaced by a naturally flushed complexion or by a mild erythematous state. It may be recalled that one of the reasons the famous arsenic-eaters of Styria reportedly took this poison (in relatively insoluble form) was to produce a rosy-healthy look. In 1873, in answer to a questionnaire which asked about some of his physical characteristics, Darwin replied that he had a "Rather sallow" complexion (F. Darwin, 1888: **3**: p. 178).

B. Arsenical melanosis is a typical condition of those who suffer from chronic arsenic intoxication. The color varies with the natural complexion of the individual. The skin is often bronzed or coppery (Du Bois and Geiling, 1959: p. 134), or deep tan, brown, or even gray or blackish. The darkest colors apparently occur in individuals having a naturally dark coloration. The pigmentation may be relieved by patches of leucoplakia (the "rain-drop appearance"). Arsenical melanosis differs from the pigmentation of Addison's disease in usually not darkening the mucous membranes. Pigmentation is commonly generalized, although areas normally exposed to light are often darker (Moeschlin, 1965: pp. 165–166; Leschke, 1934: p. 67; McNally, 1937: p. 238; Dinman, 1960: p. 138; C. K. Simpson, 1964: p. 276; Cushny, 1947: p. 168; Sollmann, 1957: p. 1204; *British Med. Jour.*, 1968: p. 191). Melanosis is common following many years of the use of arsenic (Buchanan, 1962: p. 21; *British Med. Jour.*, 1968: p. 191) and it has been reported that in the majority of cases it occurs simultaneously with the development of keratoses (Leschke, 1934: p. 67), which would mean there might be a delay of many years before the onset of the pigmentation. Vineyard workers drinking wine made from the second press of the grapes and rich in arsenic frequently observed melanoses and keratoses as the first sign of arsenic intoxication (Buchanan, 1962: pp. 25–26). A case cited by Rattner and Dorne (1943: p. 48) reveals how closely arsenical melanosis may resemble a normal suntan: a patient was taking Fowler's solution at the rate of 5 drops three times a day for 20 months for multiple sclerosis; in nine or so months it was observed that he was "suntanned"; when keratoses were noticed later it was realized that his "suntan" was instead arsenical melanosis. If Darwin's later "ruddy" complexion was truly reddish rather than bronze or coppery in hue, it could mean that he was suffering from a mild erythematous state or "flushing" which occurs in some individuals affected by chronic arsenic poisoning (Sollmann, 1957: p. 1204; Locket, 1957: p. 545; see 4-B also).

7.

A. *Vertigo; giddiness, fainting feelings,* and certain other disorders of sensation; swimming, whirling, and whizzing head (F. Darwin, 1888: **1**: p. 109, 306, 373, 379; *ibid.* **3**: p. 34, 197; Browne, 1943. p. 14; in de Beer, 1959: **2**, 1: p. 12; *British Med. Jour.,* 1882: p. 628). He also experienced buzzing, ringing, and singing in his head and black spots and stars in his eyes, and an ". . . attack of the dazzles" (F. Darwin, 1888: **1**: p. 379; *ibid.,* **3**: p. 40; Hooker, 1899: p. 188; Loewenberg, 1939: p. 53). In a notation of things to do written soon after his return from his voyage around the world, he wrote down the words, "Ear doctor" (Barlow, 1945: p. 258).

B. Leschke (1934: p. 65) and McNally (1937: pp. 237–238) emphasized vertigo, giddiness, and disturbances of vision, hearing, taste and smell as characteristic of chronic arsenic poisoning, but recent publications tend to be less specific on the matter, although terms like "disturbances of sensation" are used. A feeling of faintness is often an early sign of chronic arsenic poisoning (Du Bois and Geiling, 1959: p. 134) and in more severe cases fainting spells may occur (von Oettingen, 1958: p. 55). Vestibular toxicity and a "feeling of deafness" have been listed as a result of chronic arsenic poisoning (Vallee, Ulmer and Wacker, 1960: p. 141; Leschke, 1934: p. 65).

8.

A. *Headaches;* perhaps migraine at times (Browne, 1943: p. 14; Kohn, 1963: p. 251). ". . . almost continuous bad headache for forty-eight hours . . ." (F. Darwin, 1888: **2**: p. 323). Even as early as 1832 he speaks of having had a bad headache while in Montevideo (Barlow, 1933: p. 87).

B. Headaches may result from numerous causes, including injury to the nervous system by many different toxic agents. They are characteristic of the neurological syndrome associated with chronic arsenic intoxication, and intense persistent headaches are reportedly especially common during the advanced phases of this state (Vallee, Ulmer and Wacker, 1960: p. 141; Cushny, 1947: p. 168; Heyman, Pfeiffer, Willett and Taylor, 1956: p. 404; von Oettingen, 1958: p. 84; Locket, 1957: p. 545; Leschke, 1934: p. 65).

9.

A. *Trembling, etc.;* hands trembled at times; trembling sometimes may have been more generalized; marked deterioration of handwriting on many different occasions (de Beer, 1959: **2**, 1: p. 12; F. Darwin, 1888: **1**: p. 373). Fidgeting movements: "When walking he had a fidgeting movement with his fingers, which he described . . . as the habit of an old man;" his hand was not steady enough to cut sections of roots and leaves to be examined with the microscope, according to his son, Francis; twitching of muscle was also noted (F. Darwin, 1888: **1**: pp. 110–111, 379).

B. Disturbances of sensation and motion in localized areas are common, especially in the hands and feet; the weakness is most likely to affect the long extensors of fingers and toes. The similarity between the nerve effects of chronic alcoholism and chronic arsenic intoxication has been noted by several investigators. Tremor, motor palsy, spasms, and cramps are common manifestations. In advanced cases pseudoathetosis may appear and in very bad cases paralysis or ataxia can occur (Cushny, 1947: p. 168; Buchanan, 1962: p. 22; Vallee, Ulmer and Wacker, 1960: p. 141; Leschke, 1934: p. 65; McNally, 1937: p. 238; Heyman, Pfeiffer, Willett and Taylor, 1956: p. 405).

10.

A. *Tooth and gum problems;* five molars out at once at the age of forty-three; fairly early loss of all teeth; pyorrhea; sore gums (Browne, 1943: p. 14; F. Darwin, 1888: **1**: p. 385; Stecher, 1961: p. 203); fairly frequent reminders written by Darwin during the voyage of the *Beagle* to visit the dentist in the next port (Barlow, 1945). It has even been suggested by one source that one of Darwin's major problems was pyorrhea (see Barlow, 1958: p. 241).

B. Gums are sometimes sore and swollen in cases of chronic arsenic poisoning (Blyth and Blyth, 1920: p. 577; Locket, 1957: p. 545; Moeschlin, 1965: p. 57). Mrs. Clare Booth Luce was reported to have suffered from a bad case of chronic arsenic poisoning after ingesting large quantities of lead arsenate dust from paint in her bedroom ceiling; one of the symptoms exhibited was a loosening of her teeth (*The Lancet,* 1956: p. 182). In acute cases both gingivitis and stomatitis are common (von Oettingen, 1958: p. 65).

11.

A. *Early baldness;* Darwin mentioned growing bald at the age of twenty-eight; he was predominantly bald at thirty-three;

very bald except for the side of his head and perhaps a fringe in back a few years later (F. Darwin, 1888: 1: pp. 111, 325; Kohn, 1963: p. 243).

B. There is a tendency for hair to fall out in cases of chronic arsenic poisoning (C. K. Simpson, 1964: p. 276; McNally, 1937: pp. 238–239; Hamilton and Hardy, 1949: p. 128; *The Lancet*, 1956: p. 182; Sollmann, 1957: p. 1204). Alternatively, Darwin may have inherited the trait.

12.

A. *Arthritis; lumbago; gout;* suppressed gout; gouty constitution (Browne, 1943: p. 14; *British Med. Jour.*, 1882: p. 628; see Kohn, 1963: p. 246). Of possible relevance is Francis Darwin's description of a typical characteristic of his father: "When he sat still he often took hold of one wrist with the other hand . . ." (F. Darwin, 1888: 1: p. 111).

B. Arthralgia is a common complaint of sufferers from chronic arsenic poisoning. Acute pain is usually located around the knee, ankle or foot, and, less frequently, in the wrist or hand. In severe cases lumbar pains are mentioned as being fairly common. (Cushny, 1947: p. 168; Locket, 1957: p. 545; Dinman, 1960: p. 138; von Oettingen, 1958: p. 101; Brundage, 1913: p. 357; Bensby and Joron, 1963: p. 63; Leschke, 1934: p. 68). It might also be mentioned that another sign of peripheral neuritis resulting from chronic arsenic intoxication may be diminished tendon reflexes at the ankle, knee, wrist, and elbow (see Heyman, Pfeiffer, Willett and Taylor, 1956: p. 405, for example).

13.

A. *Bad heat control;* his son, Francis, wrote: "Two peculiarities of his indoor dress were that he almost always wore a shawl over his shoulders, and that he had great loose cloth boots lined with fur which he could slip on over his indoor shoes. Like most delicate people he suffered from heat as well as from chilliness;

it was as if he could not hit the balance between too hot and too cold . . ." (F. Darwin, 1888: **1:** p. 112; **2:** p. 27).

B. The appreciation of heat and cold and pain is often either increased or deadened among individuals suffering from chronic arsenic poisoning. Their susceptibility to cold was recognized during the last century (Buchanan, 1962: p. 23; Cushny, 1947: p. 168; Leschke, 1934: p. 65; Moeschlin, 1965: p. 165; Dinman, 1960: p. 138; Heyman, Pfeiffer, Willett and Taylor, 1956: p. 405; McNally, 1937: p. 238; Farquharson, 1880: p. 803).

14.

A. *Catarrhal problems;* Darwin was described in *The British Medical Journal* just after his death as having suffered from ". . . catarrhal dyspepsia . . ." (1882: p. 628). It is likely the source of this information was Dr. Andrew Clark. Darwin also mentioned having had a bout of pleurisy, and pleurisy and fever (Loewenberg, 1939: p. 75; F. Darwin, 1888: **2:** p. 291).

B. A catarrhal state of the exposed mucous membranes of the nose, larynx, pharynx, trachea, and bronchi are quite common in cases of chronic arsenic poisoning (Buchanan, 1962: p. 18; Leschke, 1934: p. 67; Locket, 1957: p. 546; McNally, 1937: p. 238). During part of the last century arsenic was sometimes taken as a decongestant for the mucous membranes (Aveling, 1872: p. 11).

15.

A. *"Fits";* after examining Darwin's "Dairy of health, 1849 to 1854," W. D. Foster (1965: pp. 477–478) wrote the following statement: "After the 'well very' entry, there is almost always a reference to the number of 'fits,' the nature of which is not clear, which occurred during the day and a note as to whether they were slight or bad . . . it is difficult to imagine what was the nature of the 'fits' which could be experienced every day, without ever developing into something more serious, unless they were of psychogenic origin." Darwin's grandmother, the first wife of

Dr. Erasmus Darwin, was believed by her husband to have had epilepsy-like seizures (Barlow, 1958: p. 224).

B. One of the commonly experienced symptoms of arsenical neuritis is the existence of motor and sensory sensations (sometimes pains) which may be violent in character. They are usually located initially in the hands and feet, and they then soon rise slowly up the trunk (Leschke, 1934: p. 65; McNally, 1937: p. 238; Moeschlin, 1965: p. 165). Cushny (1947: p. 168) states that in very prolonged cases of arsenic poisoning the patient may become epileptic; these symptoms usually slowly disappear when the poison is removed. Legge (discussed in Hamilton and Hardy, 1949: p. 128) examined 135 patients suffering from arsenic poisoning and found that three of them had epileptiform seizures. It is not clear whether they had been exposed to arsenic for a prolonged period. A patient who had convulsive seizures at the onset of chronic arsenic poisoning was reported by Heyman, Pfeiffer, Willett and Taylor (1956: p. 404). The term "fit" might have simply referred to periodic spasms or cramps (see 9-B); or it might have been a way of noting the number of times he had experienced an attack of vertigo (see 7-A), or had vomited (see 17-A). Alternatively, Darwin may have inherited the disability of his grandmother.

16.

A. *Heart palpitations; pain* (F. Darwin, 1888: **1:** p. 287; **3:** p. 15). "I have not been very well of late, with an uncomfortable palpitation of the heart, and my doctors urge me *strongly* to knock off all work, and go and live in the country for a few weeks [in 1837]" (F. Darwin, 1888: **1:** p. 284). His heart does not seem to have been seriously affected until his late middle age or later, however.

B. Findings within the past two decades have demonstrated a direct toxic action of arsenicals on the cardiac muscle. Butzengeiger (discussed by Buchanan, 1962: p. 17, and Moeschlin,

1965: p. 166) undertook a study of several hundred wine growers who had been exposed to arsenical insecticides for a long period of time. The electrocardiographic tracings revealed a severe departure from the normal in 28.7 per cent of the cases and less significant variations in another 15.6 per cent. During the war years, when arsenic was difficult to obtain in Germany, such findings became less frequent. In a more recent study of patients exhibiting symptoms of peripheral neuritis caused by arsenic intoxication, Heyman, Pfeiffer, Willett and Taylor (1965: p. 405) stated that of the 21 whose hearts were examined, approximately half showed ". . . various changes such as sinoatrial tachycardia, left-axis deviation, nonspecific T-wave changes and occasional ventricular extrasystoles." Vallee, Ulmer and Wacker (1960: p. 144) list palpitations resulting from anemia as one of the symptoms of chronic arsenic poisoning. Survivors of acute arsenic poisoning may reveal residual electrocardiographic changes which persist for many months (*ibid.,* p. 144; see also von Oettingen, 1958: pp. 56, 58; Blyth and Blyth, 1920: p. 578; Leschke, 1934: p. 68).

17.

A. *Nausea, vomiting, and flatulence—severe gastro-intestinal disorders.* Vomiting sometimes daily; one type of vomiting mentioned as especially bad; fear of stomach failing in public; nights always bad; wretched digestive organs (F. Darwin, 1888: **1:** pp. 334, 345–346, 381, 384, **2:** pp. 112, 132, 168, 171, 365; Browne, 1943; p. 14; Loewenberg, 1939: p. 53). Thomas Huxley recorded that during the time Darwin lived in London his frequent attacks of illness were usually accompanied by severe vomiting and great prostration of strength (cited in Kelly, 1965: p. 1128). Darwin also experienced severe attacks of flatulence at night (Browne, 1943: p. 14). "I believe I have not had one whole day, or rather night, without my stomach having been greatly disordered, during the last three years [1842–1845], and most days great prostration of strength" (F. Darwin, 1888: **1**: p. 350). From Darwin's records on his ill health, Sir Buckston Browne concluded that he had been the victim of chronic indigestion induced by five years hardship at sea (Browne, 1943: p. 15). It has recently been suggested that Darwin may have had upper intestinal tract disease (*Canadian Med. Assoc. Jour.,* 1964: p. 1371; see also Alvarez, 1943: pp. 240–243; 1959).

B. Recurrent bouts of vomiting may raise in a physician's mind a suspicion of arsenic poisoning (C. K. Simpson, 1964: pp. 274–275). Particularly severe cases may resemble gastroenteritis, dysentery, typhoid, intestinal "flu," and other similar disorders (Boos, 1939: pp. 278, 296; Sellers, 1906: p. 137). The old-time practitioners used to describe the condition as "walking typhoid" (see McNally, 1937: pp. 9–10). Violent gastroenteritis from arsenic is due to damage of the vascular bed of the tract (Bensby and Joron, 1963: p. 62). According to Leschke (1934: p. 67), in chronic arsenic poisoning, "The gastro-intestinal symptoms are, in the main, the same as acute poisoning, but with milder and protracted progress. They are characterized by . . . lack of appetite, nausea, vomiting, diarrhoea (frequently with colic), thus leading to progressive loss of weight and infirmity." Locket (1957: p. 545; see also von Oettingen, 1958: pp. 61–62) states that "Gastro-intestinal symptoms are variable and may consist merely of anorexia, minimum discomfort, and passage of occasional unformed stools. Nausea may be severe and intractable, episodes of vomiting and retching occurring irregularly." Du Bois and Geiling (1959: p. 134) mention abdominal pains, diarrhoea or constipation, or both, occurring alternately (see also Buchanan, 1962: p. 18; C. K. Simpson, 1964: p. 275; Hamilton and Hardy, 1949: p. 128; Vallee, Ulmer and Wacker, 1960: p. 141).

18.

A. *Poor and fluctuating appetite; loss of weight* (F. Darwin, 1888: **1**: pp. 350, 379; **2**: p. 91; etc.).

B. Patients with chronic arsenic poisoning usually exhibit a loss of appetite and loss of weight (Locket, 1957: p. 545; Du Bois and Geiling, 1959: p. 134; Buchanan, 1962: p. 18; C. K. Simpson, 1964: pp. 275, 277; McNally, 1937: p. 237; Leschke, 1934: p. 67; Blyth and Blyth, 1920: p. 577). Even Dr. Henry Hunt in 1844 recognized the association between arsenic taken as a medicine and a subsequent disinclination for food (1844: p. 178).

19.

A. *Chronic state of exhaustion; great prostration; insomnia; general feeling of being unwell, including mental depression and a "failure of power," formal work was limited to $1\frac{1}{2}$ to 3 hours per day during much of his adult life* (F. Darwin, 1888: **1**: pp. 109, 302, 331, 350, 381; **2**: 158, 161, 163, 171, 232, 240, 244, 359; **3**: p. 13; F. Darwin and Seward, 1903: **1**: p. 375; Hooker, 1899: p. 188; de Beer, 1959: **2**, 1: p. 12; Kelly, 1965: p. 1128). At the age of sixty, after many years of fatigue, he wrote: ". . . I have hardly crawled a mile from the house, and then have been fearfully fatigued. It is enough to make one wish oneself quiet in a comfortable tomb" (F. Darwin, 1888: **3**: p. 108). His insomnia, which was mentioned in his correspondence and in the recollections of J. D. Hooker, could have been partly related to his gastrointestinal difficulties (see 17-A).

B. Leschke's description of the common symptoms of chronic arsenic poisoning includes one which would seem to fit Darwin's case very well (1934: p. 69): "A decrease of the complete physical and mental energy and capacity for work, with fatigue and general vague ill-feeling, is often the only symptom of a chronic state of poisoning with minimum quantities of arsenic." Others have described this state as a general, classic, or vague condition of ill-health and malaise, or of weakness and prostration, or marked fatigue and mental irritability, or lack of *joie-de-vivre* (Blyth and Blyth, 1920: p. 577; Heyman, Pfeifer, Willett and Taylor, 1956: p. 403; Locket, 1957: p. 545; Buchanan, 1962: p. 18; Dinman,

1960: pp. 138, 140; Du Bois and Geiling, 1959; p. 134; Sollmann, 1957: p. 1204; Wade and Frazer, 1953: p. 269; C. K. Simpson, 1964: p. 275). Insomnia has been specifically mentioned in cases of chronic arsenic intoxication by von Oettingen (1958: p. 85) and Brundage (1913: p. 357). A picture of secondary anemia (and related cachexic states) may occur as the bone-marrow function is exhausted in patients with chronic arsenic poisoning; occasionally pernicious and aplastic anemia is seen (Leschke, 1934: p. 68; Moeschlin, 1965: p. 165; Sollmann, 1957: p. 1204; McNally, 1937: p. 238; C. K. Simpson, 1964: p. 277; see also von Oettingen, 1958: p. 119 and *The Lancet,* 1956: p. 182).

20.

A. Some *improvement in his state of health* noted after age of 63 (F. Darwin, 1888: **3**: p. 355; F. Darwin and Seward, 1903: **1**: p. 375).

B. According to Wade and Frazer (1953: p. 269), patients who had been given Fowler's solution and exhibited fairly well-developed symptoms of peripheral neuritis were reported to have completely recovered in 97 per cent of the cases studied, although a delay of two or more years sometimes elapsed before this took place. Recovery in more severe cases is normally less complete (Buchanan, 1964: p. 24): "Improvement can be expected on withdrawal from further exposure to arsenic, but is often very slow and may be incomplete, especially where motor paralyses have appeared and the muscles have given a reaction of degeneration." Damage to the liver, kidneys, heart muscle, and other vital parts may mean that a full or satisfactory recovery will never occur. It is possible that Darwin either ceased to take arsenic or significantly lessened the amount he was taking, sometime during his late middle age.

21.

A. *Death due to degeneration of the heart* and greater blood vessels (*British Med. Jour.* 1882: p. 628; see also F. Darwin, 1888: **3**: pp. 355–358; Kohn, 1963).

B. Individuals who have been subjected to a prolonged case of chronic arsenic poisoning usually die as the result of cardiac weakness associated with fatty degeneration of the heart muscle, liver, and kidneys (Du Bois and Geiling, 1959: p. 134; see C. K. Simpson, 1964: pp. 276–277; Leschke, 1934: p. 69).

The comparison between Darwin's symptoms and those manifested in chronic arsenic poisoning provides a very close match. Short of exhumation of Darwin's remains and the discovery of an abnormal thickening of the bones and the filling of the haversian canals (Sollmann, 1957: p. 1205), or some other evidence of his having taken arsenic for a long period of time,[18] the subject will never be fully closed. However, when the post-mortem picture is tied together with the medical practices of the time, and Darwin's known use and preference of arsenic to cure at least one of his troublesome and recurring ailments, the reconstruction would appear to answer all of the major problems that have been raised about the origin of his peculiar malady. Each of the matching symptoms is important, although the probable existence of multiple keratoses, his brown or coppery complexion, chronic gastro-intestinal problems, peripheral neuritis, chronic state of exhaustion, and catarrhal problems are the most significant.

[18] Individuals who have died of chronic arsenic poisoning, either during the time they were still taking arsenic, or soon thereafter, have a noticeable concentration of it in their hair and nails. It is quite possible that Darwin stopped taking arsenic a number of years before his death, as has already been suggested. If this was the case, then it is uncertain whether an analysis of his hair or nails would be of any assistance in settling the matter.

ON THE USE, DETECTION, AND LONG-TERM
EFFECTS OF ARSENIC

THE PRESENT fairly widespread aversion to the use of arsenic as a medicine arose not so very long ago. What now appears to be a rather obvious constellation of related symptoms has taken many generations to appreciate fully. There are several reasons for this.

The onset of chronic arsenic poisoning is typically gradual and insidious (see, for example, Dinman, 1960: p. 138) and the "sinister long-term effects are only just coming to be appreciated" (*British Med. Jour.* 1968: p. 191). Subjective manifestations, such as a vague malaise, ill-defined weakness, and pain in various parts of the body are common at the beginning of the illness. The time in which clear evidence of toxicity may reveal itself varies considerably with the dosage given and the level of tolerance of the individual. Some patients who had taken Fowler's solution to treat asthma exhibited toxic symptoms after a lapse of one or two years, while others did so in a few weeks (Vallee, Ulmer, and Wacker, 1960: p. 141). When arsenic has been taken for such chronic dermatoses as eczema, psoriasis, dermititis herpetiforms, lichen planus, and for various other ailments, such as migraine, epilepsy, and pernicious anemia, the result is the same (Ormsby and Montgomerey, 1954: p. 851):

. . . some patients are able to take arsenic continuously for many years with only mild pigmentation and keratoses resulting, whereas among others, marked keratoses and epitheliomas with metastasis and death result from the ingestion of very small amounts of arsenic taken many years previously.

The clinical picture is also confused by the unusual character of arsenic which may temporarily "cure" or temper the very symptoms it often produces in other individuals, or even in the same individual. It has been used as an aid to digestion, a blood and nerve tonic, and to treat skin disorders, anemia, cardiac pain, ague,

75

female complications, and many other disorders. There is little doubt that it did relieve some of these ailments. Many of the complications resulting from its administration, however, were such that they too would often have been treated by arsenic. Sir Benjamin Brodie's prescription of arsenic for certain nervous disorders has already been mentioned. He also favored its external use to destroy warts (Hawkins, 1865: p. 355), yet warts, or small keratoses, commonly result from the prolonged administration of arsenic. This is a very simple example of the multiplying series of vicious circles that must have taken place quite often and which have been discussed more fully in the earlier part of this paper (see pp. 26–28, 46–47).

Another impediment to recognition of the long-term effects of this poison is related to the widespread damage it may do to the heart, kidneys, liver, bone-marrow function, vasomotor system, and probably a number of vital enzymatic processes. A significant derangement of carbohydrate metabolism frequently reveals itself in an inhibition of the pyruvate oxidase enzyme system, producing a polyneuritis similar to that seen in thiamine deficiency (Wade and Frazer, 1953: p. 269; Moeschlin, 1965: p. 162). There is also a suggestion that the level of blood sugar may be variable and hypoglycemia may result (Sexton and Gowdey, 1947: pp. 642–643, 646). If this is substantiated by other studies it would help to explain why several of Darwin's symptoms, and those of many individuals suffering from chronic arsenicalism, partly fit into the constellations of narcolepsy, diabetogenic hyperinsulinism, and hypoglycemia (for the belief that Darwin may have been a narcoleptic, see Roberts, 1966 and 1967). Thus, heart, kidney, and liver disease, anemia, thiamine deficiency, and possibly hypoglycemia, and probably many other ailments may be caused by arsenic. Diagnostic confusion of the cause with the effect was particularly easy to make in the last century when a large number of practitioners still believed medicinal arsenic to be relatively harmless.

Doubts about the possible deleterious long-term effects of this medicine were occasionally voiced during the last century, however, but the general view favored its continued use. In 1848 the British Medical Association queried its members on the use of arsenic in skin diseases. The seventy-five answers received were reported to have emphatically testified that the remedy had never been found either fatal or permanently detrimental to health (Farquharson, 1880: p. 802). In 1863, in an article entitled, "On the question, is oxide of arsenic long used in very small quantities injurous to man?" printed in the *Edinburgh New Philosophical Journal,* it was pointed out that six families in Whitehaven in Cumberland had been drinking water from a stream charged with 1.15 grains per gallon of arsenious acid, and it did them neither harm nor good—only their ducks invariably died from its effect (Stockman, 1902: p. 1228). The often-reported case of the Styrian peasants consuming quantities of arsenic (later found to have been taken in relatively insoluble form) also helped to diminish the doubts of some of the practitioners.

In England at the turn of the century arsenic was accidentally introduced into a commercial beer and widespread chronic arsenical symptoms, such as peripheral neuritis, occurred. Questions were once again raised about the medicine, but many remained unconvinced and continued to prescribe it. Ralph Stockman, writing in *The British Medical Journal* in 1902 (1902: pp. 1227–1228) was one of these. He emphasized the great value of this drug in curing skin diseases:

> The slighter symptoms of arsenical poisoning such as gastric disturbances, irritation of the eyes, oedema of the eyelids are familiar enough, but these pass off rapidly on stopping the administration or lessening the dose, and as they leave behind no ill-effects they can hardly be described as more than a temporary inconvenience. I am in the habit of prescribing arsenical preparations freely, seldom in extreme doses (15 minims liquor arsenicalis or $\frac{1}{8}$ gr. arsenious acid daily being about the upward limit, although I do occasionally use very much stronger doses) and I have never seen any untoward effects more serious than slight symptoms of commencing peripheral neuritis, some pigmentation of the skin, . . . or trifling eruptions, all of which readily disappear without treatment.

A colleague of his, Frank M. Pope, wrote at the same time in the same journal advocating the continued use of arsenic for chorea (*ibid.,* p. 1230). The first step he recommended was to give the patient a mild mercurial and put him on a bland and easily digested diet. For adults this should then be followed by two or three ounces of liquor arsenicalis three times a day, increasing the dosage daily by $2\frac{1}{2}$ minims. His philosophy was to create a ". . . shock action on the nerve tissues." If unpleasant symptoms developed they should be more or less ignored:

> Do not discontinue on the first attack of vomiting. This is often due to accidental causes, and the patient may be able to go for two or three days without a recurrence.
>
> . . . . .
>
> If the vomiting persists, discontinue the drug for 24 hours, and then give the same dose as the last.

Even as late as 1955 it was stated in a semi-popular book on poisons that (Schenk, 1955: p. 108):

> Medicinal arsenic taken at the rate of half to five milligrams daily is an aid to the human combustion and anabolism. A course of arsenic extending over several months is an effective treatment for general debility and nervous exhaustion.

It is still used to treat skin diseases, although this is done with more caution than before (see Wiener, 1955, for example). Even so, there is abundant evidence that in the past several decades much harm has been done by this medication. In 1947 and 1957 two investigators separately collected a combined total of 180 cases from the literature in which skin cancer had been attributed to the medicinal use of arsenic (see Bonser, 1967: p. 129). As late as 1967 M. M. Black wrote that Fowler's solution in "conventional doses" was still being given for several types of skin ailments and in smaller doses as a general skin and blood tonic (*British Med. Jour.* 1968: p. 191). In commenting on this fact, the editor of *The British Medical Journal* for 1968 warned: "As it is not yet known whether any dose of arsenic, however small, is safe, such empirical prescribing should be condemned" (*ibid.,* p. 191).

"FOWLER'S DISEASE"—A PROBABLE
VICTORIAN MALADY

If the prescription of arsenic was as common during the nineteenth century as the medical reports of the time would seem to suggest, it would be expected that many individuals were victim of the long-term effects of chronic arsenic poisoning. Insofar as the tradition of using arsenic as a daily prophylactic against the ague was firmly established for a long period of time in the "fenny parts" of England, it is likely that some of the residents of places like Cambridgeshire developed chronic symptoms.[19] A study of the health records of that period might turn up some interesting facts. The use of arsenic in all parts of Great Britain against a multitude of disorders must also have left large numbers of people suffering from what might be called "Fowler's disease." The possibility that many patients, who were classed as "dyspeptics" or "hypochondriacs," may have been suffering from this form of medication or even a complex of different types of chronic poisoning is worth consideration. Certainly the famous dyspeptics already mentioned—Thomas De Quincey, Thomas Carlyle and his wife, Robert Browning, George Lewes, Margaret Fuller Ossoli, Herbert Spencer, Thomas Huxley, George Eliot, and Charles Darwin[20]—manifested many of the same symptoms. The assertion is even more convincing if one compares Sir James Clark's list of symptoms typical of atonic and nervous dyspeptics in the latter part of

[19] Darwin's dark-complexioned professor of geology at Cambridge, Adam Sedgwick, might have been one such example. He suffered from a variety of ailments during most of his adult life. The symptoms included "gout," rheumatic attacks, indigestion, "nervousness," and vague symptoms which his friends sometimes were said to have identified as mental rather than physical (see Fenton and Fenton, 1952: p. 110; Clark and Hughes, 1890: **1**: p. 379).

[20] In the United States the enigmatic and prolonged sickness of Francis Parkman (author of *The Oregon Trail*) somewhat resembled Darwin's syndrome of complaints: he had chronic diarrhea, arthritic complaints, insomnia, conjunctivitis and various crises which apparently manifested themselves in the form of vomiting and boils (Atwater, 1967: pp. 429, 432).

the first half of the last century, with the symptoms of chronic arsenic poisoning, as shown in the following list, in which items indicated by "A" are taken from Clark (1846) and "B" from the literature on chronic arsenic poisoning. Symptoms which Darwin had are indicated.

1.

A. Little or variable appetite; sometimes a loathing toward food.

B. Common, see 18-B of former table, p. 72. The first part applies to Darwin, see 18-A. p. 71.

2.

A. Disturbed sleep.

B. Apparently common, see 19-B, p. 72. Applies to Darwin, see 19-A, p. 72.

3.

A. Headaches; at times sudden; sometimes preceded by no. 4 (to follow).

B. Fairly common, see 8-B, p. 65. Applies to Darwin, See 8-A, p. 65.

4.

A. Sense of coldness and creeping on the surface; sometimes preceded by no. 5 (to follow).

B. There appears to be no specific mention of this symptom although "temperature sensations" in the hands, feet and lower legs in a "symmetrical stocking-glove" distribution are apparently common (see, for example, Heyman, Pfeiffer, Willett and Taylor, 1956: p. 405).

5.

A. Numbness in the extremities and no. 6 (to follow).

B. Fairly common (Locket, 1957; p. 545; Moeschlin, 1965: p. 165; Blyth and Blyth, 1920: p. 577; Heyman, Pfeiffer, Willett and Taylor, 1956: p. 405).

6.

A. Dimness of vision and other ocular spectra or no. 7. (to follow).

B. See 7-B, p. 64, and the sources listed (Moeschlin, 1965: p. 165; Vallee, Ulmer, and Wacker, 1960: p. 141; Heyman, Pfeiffer, Willett and Taylor, 1956: p. 404; Sollmann, 1957: p. 1204). Darwin reported experiencing ocular spectra, see 7-A, p. 64.

7.

A. Uneasy sensation originating in one of the extremities and gradually ascending to the head resembling "the aura epileptica."

B. See 15-B, p. 69; also no. 7-B, p. 64. This possibly applies to Darwin, see 15-A, p. 68.

8.

A. Nausea or vomiting in some individuals; gastric complaints; epigastric pain; diarrhea and sometimes constipation; "great distension" and "fetid eructations."

B. Common, see 17-B, p. 71. Most of this applies to Darwin, see 17-A, p. 70.

9.

A. "Strong mental impressions" occur with the air of crowded rooms.

B. Mental disturbances not infrequently occur, although severe mental disorders are rare—the principal exception being with individuals who consume alcohol in any quantity. Personality changes have also been noted. Darwin studiously avoided crowded conditions, although this may have been for physical as well as for psychological reasons. (Moeschlin, 1965: p. 166;

Leschke, 1934: pp. 65, 68–69; Vallee, Ulmer and Wacker, 1960: p. 141; Heyman, Pfeiffer, Willett and Taylor, 1956: p. 403). This may also refer to the kinds of disturbances discussed in 7-B, p. 64.

10.

A. Disposition to chilliness.

B. Common, see 13-B, p. 68. Applies to Darwin, see 13-A, p. 67.

11.

A. Cramps. (Clark relates this to eating indigestible food.)

B. Both colic and muscular cramps. See 9-B and 17-B, pp. 66, 71 (Hamilton and Hardy, 1949: p. 128; Heyman, Pfeiffer, Willett and Taylor, 1956: p. 405). This might apply to Darwin, see 17-A, p. 70.

12.

A. Vertigo and faintness.

B. See 7-B, p. 64. Applies to Darwin, see 7-A, p. 64.

13.

A. "Clammy perspirations."

B. One of the vasomotor disorders associated with chronic arsenic poisoning is sweating. Feverishness and drenching sweats have also been mentioned (Sollmann, 1957: p. 1204; Heyman, Pfeiffer, Willet and Taylor, 1956: p. 404).

14.

A. Paralysis.

B. Common in advanced cases (Sollmann, 1957: p. 1204; Cushny, 1947: p. 168; Leschke, 1934: pp. 65–66; McNally, 1937: p. 238). Darwin's father was reported to have warned his son that if he continued to take arsenic he ran the risk of becoming partially paralyzed.

15.

A. Loss of voice.

B. According to Sollmann (1957: p. 1204) the voice may be altered by paralysis of the vocal cords.

16.

A. Partial loss of sight.

B. See 7-B, p. 64.

17.

A. Loss of smell.

B. According to Moeschlin (1965: pp. 165–166) a comparatively common disturbance (see also Leschke, 1934: p. 65).

18.

A. Deafness.

B. See 7-B, p. 64.

19.

A. Asthma.

B. There appears to be no specific mention of asthma being associated with chronic arsenic intoxication. Bronchitis is fairly common in such cases, however; see 14-B, p. 68.

20.

A. Spasmodic cough.

B. Common, see 14-B, p. 68 and the sources listed (Moeschlin, 1965: p. 165; Du Bois and Geiling, 1959: p. 134; Cushny, 1947: p. 167; Vallee, Ulmer and Wacker, 1960: p. 141; Heyman, Pfeiffer, Willett and Taylor, 1956: p. 404).

21.

A. Various skin affections.

B. Common, see 1-B through 5-B, pp. 59–62. Applies to Darwin, see 1-A through 5-A, pp. 59–62.

22.

A. Various affections of the joints.

B. Fairly common, see 12-B, p. 67. Applies to Darwin see 12-A, p. 67.

23.

A. Various affections of the nervous system.

B. Common. See many of the symptoms indicated by B in this list and the one beginning on p. 59. Applies to Darwin.

24.

A. Palpitations.

B. See 16-B, p. 69. Applies to Darwin, see 16-A, p. 69.

25.

A. Convulsive affections.

B. See 15-B, p. 69. Possibly applies to Darwin, see 15-A, p. 68.

26.

A. Tic douloureux.

B. Rare cases of pain of the facial nerves have been reported (Moeschlin, 1965: p. 165).

27.

A. Headache (repeat of 3-A of this list).

B. See 3-B of this list and 8-B, p. 65. Applies to Darwin.

CONCLUSION

Darwin's so-called dyspeptic and hypochondriacal symptoms were therefore by no means unique in the age to which he belonged. Nor was his associated pattern of behavior unusual. His move from London to Down to escape the "unhealthy airs" of London and the stress of London society were probably due to the urging of his two doctors. He had in fact entertained the idea of living in the country for many years before his move. His general avoidance of society was necessitated by the frequency and unpredictability of the various ailments that afflicted him for many years, and his tendency to develop vasomotor and gastrointestinal symptoms when excited or upset. His chronic state of fatigue and weakness and inability to work long at a time are typical of "Fowler's disease." The suspicion held by doctors and friends that he may have been a hypochondriac must have placed an additional burden upon him. With minor modification, these points also apply to his friend, Thomas Huxley, and to George Eliot, and probably to a number of other people—prominent and otherwise—during the Victorian era.

The issue whether Darwin's state of ill health was primarily psychogenic or physical is not an academic one. In many ways Darwin's approach to scientific questions was a reflection of his unique personality. Many naturalists and scientists had traveled to the distant reaches of the earth before Darwin ever set foot aboard the H.M.S. *Beagle,* but none of them had seen or thought about the world in the same way as he did. The difference was qualitative. The widely held belief that he was inspired and motivated, directly or indirectly, in his life's work by sublimated hatreds and guilt-feelings has been based in large part upon the supposed psychosomatic character of his ill health and upon highly tenuous reasoning. The very high probability that he was the victim of chronic arsenic poisoning, possibly complicated by other forms of treatment,[21] permits one to look elsewhere for an explanation. It also frees the mind from the burden of presupposing an ulterior design of many of his thoughts and ideas. The people who knew him well remembered him as an open, unassuming, affectionate, generous, and contagiously enthusiastic individual who expressed a deep love for the earth and the life it supports.

---

[21] Colocynth, colchicum, gamboge, iodide of potassium, opium, strychnine, and calomel (mercurous chloride) are a few of the many potentially toxic medicines he might have taken throughout much of his life. It took a great many years to appreciate the long-term effects of arsenic. Nothing is known about the long-term effects of arsenic and calomel taken together, and this was a common practice then. It is possible, also, that the prolonged and liberal use of calomel and other closely related inorganic mercurial preparations, even when not taken with arsenic, may have done long-lasting damage to certain individuals. This especially applies to young children who sometimes develop acrodynia, or pink disease, which is characterized by some of the following signs and symptoms: erythema, mental disturbances, irritability, insomnia, sweating, disordered sensation of the extremities, peripheral vascular phenomena, anorexia, weakness, photophobia, tachycardia, gingivitis, red hands and feet that are swollen and cold, loss of teeth and hair, and a slight fever (Bidstrup, 1964: p. 31). It may be wondered whether the exceptionally large and frequent doses of calomel prescribed by doctors during Darwin's lifetime might not have stricken some hypersensitive adults with pink disease.

REFERENCES CITED

ADLER, S. 1959. "Darwin's Illness." *Nature* **184**, 4693: pp. 1102–1103.
—— 1965. "Darwin's Illness." *Brit. Med. Jour.*, 5444: pp. 1249–1250.
ALVAREZ, W. C. 1943. *Nervous Indigestion and Pain* (New York, Harper & Brothers Publishers).
—— 1959. "The Nature of Charles Darwin's Lifelong Ill-Health." *New Eng. Jour. Med.* **261**: pp. 1109–1112.
ATWATER, E. C. 1967. "The Lifelong Sickness of Francis Parkman (1823–93)." *Bull. Hist. Med.* **41**, 5: pp. 413–439.
AVELING, J. H. 1872. "The Value of Arsenic in Menorrhagia." *Brit. Med. Jour.* (1): pp. 10–11.
BARLOW, NORA (ed.) 1933. *Charles Darwin's Diary* (Cambridge, The University Press).
—— (ed.) 1945. *Charles Darwin and The Voyage of the Beagle* (London, Pilot Press Ltd.).
—— 1954. "The Life of the Shawl." *Lancet* **266**: pp. 414–415.
—— (ed.) 1958. *The Autobiography of Charles Darwin, 1809–1882* (London, Collins).
—— (ed.) 1967. *Darwin and Henslow, The Growth of an Idea* (London, Bentham-Moxon Trust, and John Murray).
DE BEER, (Sir) G. (ed.) 1959. "Darwin's Journal." *Bull. Brit. Mus. (Nat. Hist.)*, *Hist. Ser.* **2**, 1: pp. 1–21.
—— (ed.) 1968. "The Darwin Letters at Shrewsbury School." *Notes and Rec., Roy. Soc. London.* **23**, 1: pp. 68–85.
BEERMAN, H. 1946. "Tumors of the Skin, Part I—A Review of Recent Literature." *Amer. Jour. Med. Sci.* **211**: pp. 480–504.
BENSBY, E. H., and G. E. JORON. 1963. *Handbook of Treatment of Acute Poisoning* (3rd ed.) (Baltimore, Williams and Wilkins Company).
BERDOE, E. 1893. *The Origin and Growth of the Healing Art* (London, Swan Sonnenschein & Co.).
BIBBY, C. 1959. *T. H. Huxley* (New York, Horizon Press).
BIDSTRUP, P. L. 1964. *Toxicity of Mercury and Its Compounds* (Amsterdam, Elsevier Publishing Company).
BLYTH, A., and M. W. BLYTH. 1920. *Poisons: Their Effects and Detection* (5th ed. rev.) (London, Charles Griffin & Company, Limited).
BONSER, G. M. 1967. "Cancer Hazards of the Pharmacy." *Brit. Med. Jour.* (1), 5572: pp. 129–134.
BOOS, W. F. 1939. *The Poison Trail* (Boston, Cushman & Flint).
British Medical Journal. 1882. "The Late Charles Darwin." *Brit. Med. Jour.* (1): p. 628.
—— 1968. "Arsenic and Cancer." *Brit. Med. Jour.* (1): p. 191.
BROWNE, (Sir) B. 1943. "Darwin's Health." *Nature* **151**, 3818: pp. 14–15.
BRUNDAGE, A. H. 1913. *A Manual of Toxicology* (7th ed. rev.) (London, Baillière, Tindall & Cox).
BUCHANAN, W. D. 1962. *Toxicity of Arsenic Compounds* (Amsterdam, Elsevier Publishing Company).
Canadian Medical Association Journal. 1964. "Darwin's Illness." *Can. Med. Ass. Jour.* **91**: pp. 1371–1372.
CLARK, A. 1881. "Dr. Andrew Clark on Alcohol." *Brit. Med. Jour.*: pp. 90–91.

CLARK, J. 1846. *The Sanative Influence of Climate* (4th ed.) (London, John Murray).

CLARK, J., and T. M. HUGHES (eds.) 1890. *The Life and Letters of The Reverend Adam Sedgwick* (2 v., Cambridge, The University Press).

CUSHNY, A. R. 1947. *Pharmacology and Therapeutics* (13th ed. rev., by A. Grollman and D. Slaughter) (Philadelphia, Lea & Febiger).

DARLINGTON, C. D. 1959. *Darwin's Place in History* (Oxford, Basil Blackwell).

DARWIN, C. R. var. dates. Darwin Papers (unpublished, Anderson Room, University Library, University of Cambridge), No. 112.

―――― 1842. "Notes on the Effects Produced by the Ancient Glaciers of Caernarvonshire, and on the Boulders Transported by Floating Ice." *Edin. New Phil. Jour.* 33: pp. 352–363.

DARWIN, F. (ed.) 1888. *The Life and Letters of Charles Darwin* (3 v., London, John Murray).

DARWIN F., and A. C. SEWARD (eds.). 1903. *More Letters of Charles Darwin* (2 v., London, John Murray).

DINMAN, B. D. 1960. "Arsenic: Chronic Human Intoxication." *Jour. Occ. Med.* (March): pp. 137–141.

DU BOIS, K. P., and E. M. K. GEILING. 1959. *Textbook of Toxicology* (New York, Oxford University Press).

DUNCAN, A., JR. 1804. *The Edinburgh New Dispensatory* (2nd ed.) (Edinburgh, Printed for Bell & Bradfute).

FARQUHARSON, R. 1880. "On the Use of Arsenic in Skin-Diseases." *Brit. Med. Jour.* (1): pp. 802–804.

FENTON, C. L., and M. A. FENTON. 1952. *Giants of Geology* (Garden City, Dolphin Books, Doubleday & Company, Inc.).

FORSTER, G. 1777. *A Voyage Round the World* (2 v., London, B. White).

FOSTER, W. D. 1965. "A Contribution to the Problem of Darwin's Ill-Health." *Bull. Hist. Med.* 39, 5: pp. 476–478.

GETZELS, J. W., and M. CSIKSZENTMIHALYI. 1967. "Scientific Creativity." *Sci. Jour.* 3, 9: pp. 80–84.

GIOVACCHINI, P. L. 1960. "On Scientific Creativity." *Jour. Psychoanal. Ass.* 8: pp. 407–426.

GOOD, R. 1954a. "The Life of the Shawl." *Lancet* 266, 1: pp. 106–107.

―――― 1954b. "The Origin of *The Origin:* a Psychological Approach." *Biol. and Hum. Af.* 20, 1: pp. 10–16.

GOULD, G. M. 1903–1904. *Biographical Clinics* (3 v., Philadelphia, P. Blakiston's Son & Co.).

GREENACRE, P. 1963. *The Quest for the Father* (New York, International Universities Press, Inc.).

HAMILTON, A., and H. L. HARDY. 1949. *Industrial Toxicology* (New York, Paul B. Hoeber, Inc.).

HAWKINS, C. (ed.) 1865. *The Works of Sir Benjamin Collins Brodie* (3 v., London, Longman, Green, Longman, Roberts, & Green).

HEYMAN, A., J. B. PFEIFFER, JR., R. W. WILLETT, and H. M. TAYLOR. 1956. "Peripheral Neuropathy Caused by Arsenical Intoxication." *New Eng. Jour. Med.* 254, 9: pp. 401–409.

HOLLAND, H. 1840. *Medical Notes and Reflections* (2nd ed.) (London, Longman, Orme, Brown, and Longman).

HOOKER, J. D. 1899. "Reminiscences of Darwin." *Nature* 60, 1547: pp. 187–188.

HUBBLE, D. 1943. "Charles Darwin and Psychotherapy." *Lancet* 244, 1: pp. 129–133.

―――― 1946. "The Evolution of Charles Darwin." *Horizon* 14, 80: pp. 74–85.

―――― 1953. "The Life of the Shawl." *Lancet* 265, 6800: pp. 1351–1354.

HUDSON, L. 1966. *Contrary Imaginations, A Psychological Study of the English Schoolboy* (London, Methuen & Co. Ltd.).

HUNT, H. 1844. *On the Nature and Treatment of Tic Douloureux, Sciatica, and Other Neuralgic Disorders* (London, John Churchill).

—— 1854. *On the Severer Forms of Heartburn and Indigestion, Especially those which arise from Constitutional Causes* (London, John Churchill).

HUTCHINSON, J. 1887. "Arsenic Cancer." *Brit. Med. Jour.* (2): pp. 1280–1281.

HUXLEY, L. (ed.). 1900. *Life and Letters of Thomas Henry Huxley* (2 v., New York, Appleton and Company).

JOHNSTON, W. W. 1901. "The Ill Health of Charles Darwin: Its Nature and Its Relation to His Work." *Amer. Anthrop.* (n.s.) 3: pp. 139–158.

JONES, E. 1959. *Free Associations; Memories of a Psycho-Analyst* (New York, Basic Books, Inc., Publishers).

KELLY, M. 1964. "Robert Darwin's Splendid Character." *Isis* 55, 179: pp. 74–79.

—— 1965. "Darwin's Illness." *Brit. Med. Jour.* (2): p. 1128.

—— 1967. "Darwin Really was Sick." *Jour. Chron. Dis.* 20: p. 341.

KEMPF, E. J. 1920. *Psychopathology* (St. Louis, C. V. Mosby Company).

KING, P. P. 1839. *Proceedings of the First Expedition, 1826–30* (v. 1 of "Narrative of the Surveying Voyages of His Majesty's Ships *Adventure* and *Beagle*) (London, Henry Colburn).

KOHN, L. A. 1963. "Charles Darwin's Chronic Ill Health." *Bull. Hist. Med.* 37, 3: pp. 239–256.

Lancet. 1956. "Arsenic in the House." *Lancet* 271, 2: pp. 182–183.

LESCHKE, E. 1934. *Clinical Toxicology* (trans. C. P. Stewart and O. Dorrer) (Baltimore, William Wood & Company).

LITCHFIELD, H. (ed.). 1915. *Emma Darwin, A Century of Family Letters, 1792–1896* (2 v., London, John Murray).

LOCKET, S. 1957. *Clinical Toxicology* (St. Louis, C. V. Mosby Company).

LOEWENBERG, B. J. (ed.). 1939. *Calendar of the Letters of Charles Darwin to Asa Gray* (Historical Records Survey, Division of Professional and Service Projects, U. S. Works Project Administration, Massachusetts).

LONGFORD, E. 1964. *Victoria R. I.* (London, Weidenfeld & Nicolson).

LYELL, K. (ed.). 1881. *Life, Letters and Journals of Sir Charles Lyell, Bart.* (2 v., London, John Murray).

McNALLY, W. D. 1937. *Toxicology* (Chicago, Industrial Medicine).

MEDAWAR, P. 1967. *The Art of the Soluble* (London, Methuen & Co. Ltd.).

METTLER, C. C., and F. A. METTLER (eds.). 1947. *History of Medicine* (Philadelphia, Blakiston Company).

MOESCHLIN, S. 1965. *Poisoning, Diagnosis and Treatment* (trans. J. Bickel, 4th German ed.) (New York, Grune & Stratton).

MORETON, A. L. 1921. "Correspondence." *Ann. Med. Hist.* 3: p. 89.

VON OETTINGEN, W. F. 1958. *Poisoning; A Guide to Clinical Diagnosis and Treatment* (2nd ed., Philadelphia, W. B. Saunders Company).

ORMSBY, O. S., and H. MONTGOMEREY. 1954. *Diseases of the Skin* (8th ed., Philadelphia, Lea & Febiger).

OSBORN, H. F. 1909. "Life and Works of Darwin." *Pop. Sci. Mon.:* pp. 315–343.

POPE, F. M. 1902. "Arsenic in the Treatment of Chorea." *Brit. Med. Jour.* (2): pp. 1229–1230.

RATTNER, H., and M. DORNE. 1943. "Arsenical Pigmentation and Keratoses." *Arch. Derm. and Syph.* 48: pp. 458–459.

ROBERTS, H. J. 1966. "Reflections on Darwin's Illness." *Jour. Chron. Dis.* 19: pp. 723–725.

—— 1967. "Reflections on Darwin's Illness." *Geriatrics* 22, 9: pp. 160–168.

ROE, A. 1953. "A Psychological Study of Eminent Psychologists and Anthropologists, and a Comparison with Biological and Physical Scientists." *Psych. Mon.: Gen. Appl.* 67, 352: pp. 1–55.

ROMANES, G. J. 1882. "Charles Darwin, I." *Nature* 26: pp. 49–51.

ROSENBLOOM, J. 1919. "An Appreciation of Henry Bence Jones, M.D., F.R.S. (1814–1873)." *Ann. Med. Hist.* 2: pp. 262–264.

SCHENK, G. 1955. *The Book of Poisons* (trans. M. Ballock, German) (New York, Rinehart & Company, Inc.).

SELLERS, W. 1906. *A Handbook of Legal Medicine* (Manchester, The University Press).

SEXTON, G. B., and C. W. GOWDEY. 1947. "Relation between Thiamine and Arsenic Toxicity." *Arch. Derm. Syph.* 56, 5: pp. 634–647.

SIMPSON, C. K. 1964. *Forensic Medicine* (5th ed.) (London, Edward Arnold, Publications).

SIMPSON, G. G. 1958. "Charles Darwin in Search of Himself." *Sci. Amer.* 199, 2: pp. 117–122.

SOLLMANN, T. 1957. *A Manual of Pharmacology* (8th ed.) (Philadelphia, W. B. Saunders Company).

STECHER, R. M. (ed.) 1961. "The Darwin-Innes Letters." *Ann. Sci.* 17, 4: pp. 201–258.

STETTEN, D. 1959. "Gout." *Per. in Biol. and Med.* 2, 2: pp. 185–196.

STOCKMAN, R. 1902. "The Therapeutic Value of Arsenic and the Justification of its Continued Use in the Light of Recent Observations Concerning its Toxic Action." *Brit. Med. Jour.* 2: pp. 1227–1229.

VALLEE, B. L., D. D. ULMER, and W. E. C. WACKER. 1960. "Arsenic Toxicology and Biochemistry." *A. M. A. Arch. of Ind. Health* 21, 2: pp. 132–151.

WADE, H. J., and E. S. FRAZER. 1953. "Toxipathic Hepatitis Due to Fowler's Solution." *Lancet* 264, 1: pp. 269–271.

WIENER, K. 1955. *Systemic Associations and Treatment of Skin Diseases* (St. Louis, C. V. Mosby Company).

WILDER, A. 1901. *History of Medicine* (New Sharon, New England Eclectic Publ. Co.).

WILSON, T. G. 1946. *Victorian Doctor* (New York, L. B. Fischer).

WOODRUFF, A. W. 1965. "Darwin's Health in Relation to His Voyage to South America." *Brit. Med. Jour.*: pp. 745–750.

———— 1968. "The Impact of Darwin's Voyage to South America on His Work and Health." *Bull. N. Y. Acad. Sci.* 44: 6: pp. 661–672.

INDEX

Addison's disease, 63
Adler, S., 8, 47, 51
Alcohol, medical usage of, 34
Alvarez, W. C., 47, 71
Antimonials, medical usage of, 37
Arnica, tincture of, Darwin's use, 45
Arsenic, Darwin's use of, 5, 43–45, 52, 58–59; medical usage of (see, also, Fowler's solution), 5, 26–28, 30, 31, 34, 43–47, 52, 64: symptoms of intoxication, 27, 28, 59–74, 76
Ascencion Island, 50
Atwater, E. C., 79
Aveling, J. H., 68

Barlow, N., 43, 47, 61
Baths, cold, use of in medicine, 26
Beagle, H.M.S., 1, 2, 5, 21, 24, 43, 47, 48, 52, 54, 56, 66, 85
de Beer, G., 59, 64
Beerman, H., 47, 59
Benchuca bug (see Chagas's disease)
Bensby, E. H., and G. E. Joron, 67, 71
Berdoe, E., 32
Bibby, C., 6
Bidstrup, P. L., 86
Biett, L.-T., 46
Black, M. M., 78
Blistering, medical practice of, 30
Bloodletting, medical practice of, 26, 29, 36–37
Blyth, A., and M. W. Blyth, 47, 59, 66, 70, 72, 81
Bonser, G. M., 78
Boos, W. F., 46, 71
Brazil, 15, 54, 55, 60
Brinton, W., 31–32, 51
British Medical Association, 77
British Medical Journal, 34, 45, 59, 62, 63, 64, 67, 73, 75, 77, 78
Brodie, B., 30, 32, 76
Browne, B., 59, 64, 65, 66, 67, 70, 71
Browning, R., 35, 79
Brundage, A. H., 67, 73
Buchanan, W. D., 47, 59, 62, 63, 64, 66, 68, 69, 71, 72, 73
Buenos Aires, 55
Burt, C., 7

Butler, S., 10
Bynoe, B., 56

Calomel, 26, 27, 29, 36, 37, 56, 86
Cambridge, 1, 29, 44, 46, 48, 58, 79
Canadian Medical Association Journal, 71
Cape Verde Islands, 15
Carlyle, T., 35, 79
Chagas's disease, theory of the origin of Darwin's ill-health, 8, 47, 51
Cinnamon, medical usage of (see, also, Fowler's solution), 26, 46, 55, 56
Clark, A., 2, 32–34, 35, 39, 41, 68
Clark, J., 1, 2, 24, 26, 33, 79, 80
Climate and disease, 2–3
Colchicum, medical usage of, 29, 30, 86
Colocynth, medical usage of, 30, 86
Copper, sulphate of, medical usage, 29
Cumberland, 77
Cushny, A. R., 60, 63, 65, 66, 67, 68, 69, 82, 83

Darlington, C. D., 6
Darwin, Caroline, 14, 55
Darwin, C. R., psychogenic interpretations of the origin of his ill-health, 4–19, 58, 85
    publications of, *Autobiography,* 7; coral reef study, 16; glaciation of Wales, 50; *Journal of Researches,* 2, 16; *The Origin of Species,* 2, 6, 16; terraces of Glenroy, 16
    purchase of medicines (see arsenic), 43–45, 52, 56, 57
    question of his suffering from hypochondria, 20–23
    suggested causes of his ill-health: appendicitis, 47; brucellosis, 47; Chagas's disease, 8, 47, 51; duodenal ulcer, 47; gout, 47; hypoglycemia, 76; malaria, 47; narcolepsy, 76; neurasthenia, 47; peptic ulcer, 47; pyorrhea, 47; seasickness, 47, 71; upper intestinal tract disease, 71
    symptoms relating to his ill-health: appetite, poor, 71; arthritis, 67; auditory problems, 64; baldness,